TRA

WITH

MR TURNER

NIGEL C WINTER

Panther Publishing

Published by Panther Publishing Ltd in 2011
Panther Publishing Ltd
10 Lime Avenue
High Wycombe
Buckinghamshire HP11 1DP
www.panther-publishing.com

ISBN 978-0-9564975-4-3

DEDICATION

This book is dedicated to the men and women of the Meriden Workers' Co-operative...and indeed all those who keep the legend alive.

ACKNOWLEDGEMENTS

Authors (if I can consider myself one of this body of people) really owe most gratitude to you the reader. Particularly if you buy this book. More so if you buy two copies. Best of all if you pop in to your local public library and challenge them with a book they haven't got on their shelves because, I am told, they might go out and order lots of copies. So if you do any of these things I would like to express my sincere gratitude. Thank you.

I also owe a debt of gratitude to the most eclectic mix of minor to increasingly major (by my standards) public figures. I am going to make the most out of this so brace yourself. First of all I would like to thank Mr John Nelson, the former general manager of Triumph Motorcycles of Meriden, who quite incredibly found the photographs of the original ride around which this book is based. All of the pictures of the original ride that became known as the Gaffers' Gallop are from Mr Nelson's own archive and these are situated at the start of the chapters (with the exception of the photos at the start of the chapters *The End, The Victoria Inn, The Crown and Mitre* and *Two Years Later* which are my own).

Then there's the World Speed Record holder Norman Hyde, a constant supporter and a man with a sense of humour. Ted Simon the author, in the midst of his wedding plans, granted me kind permission to quote a large chunk from his classic tome. And then there's the approachable Rt Hon Tony Benn, for his few kind words at the start of this book. Moving now into the realms of superstardom, I am indebted to Ian Anderson of Jethro Tull for his kind permission to quote the lyrics of *Too Old To Rock 'n' Roll Too Young To Die,* that appear within these pages. Just when it appears that it can't get any better I would like to thank Don Brown formerly of Johnson Motors in California. Don, a friend of the late great Steve McQueen (of The Great Escape fame and much else) sold Steve his first Triumph and gave me much first hand detail of how this iconic motorcycle became linked to the 'King Of Cool'.

I know. All too much.

Coming back down to earth now. There's a plethora of publishers and authors whose works have been quoted within these pages. So many in fact that I have a separate section of Notes at the back of this book. Without these highly literate individuals these pages would lack the colour and vibrancy that their words have added.

No acknowledgement would be complete without mentioning the author's Mum and Dad. It was my Dad's photograph album that encouraged me to go places on motorcycles and my Mum's home cooking that ensured that I always came back.

At the outset, the trip around which this book is based had a charitable purpose. Those many that made personal donations did so without a desire for any public recognition for their generosity. They all know who they are and I, at least, am grateful to them. I also had a range of corporate sponsors including Avon Tyres, Norman Hyde Enterprises Limited, UKBiker, OKO, Scottoiler, The Motorcycle Workshop, The National Motorcycle Museum and Bob Heath Visors. Thank you all.

I would also add to this list Edward Turner's biographer, the late Jeff Clew, who provided his kind and wise counsel in those distant days when this book was but an idea. I am naturally saddened that he did not see the product of his encouragement.

By now I should be thanking my publisher Rollo Turner. All of my dealings with Rollo have left me questioning why I ever wanted to join the literati.

Despite being a lawyer myself, I was surprised at the amount of 'law' there is to writing a book and I was lucky enough to be able to call upon Anna Ganley at the Society Of Authors.

Finally my long suffering wife Tilly and our son Benedict kept the home fires burning that rainy morning, one day in June, when I rode out of their lives, dressed like a trawler man. And rode back a week or so later in possibly an even worse state.

Edward Turner, the man behind Triumph motorcycles

CONTENTS

FOREWORD

The Co-operative was a classic struggle that entered into the annals of the labour movement and which this book will help us understand.

The Rt Hon Tony Benn

THE END

I was fifty-four years late for my meeting with Mr Turner. Still, I had a photograph of our rendezvous that I had looked at many times. I had imagined what it would be like to stand in the very spot where he had stood, having done exactly what he had done and look back at the camera, and now I was moments from doing just that.

Mr Turner built the motorcycle that put Steve McQueen over the wire in *The Great Escape*. He mobilised the Rockers of the sixties and when the police could not catch them, they turned to Mr Turner for faster cars, as indeed did public figures as diverse as the Queen and the Kray Twins. But it is his Triumph motorcycles for which Mr Turner is most famous, enjoying a production run of seventy-five years if you are not too fussy about detail. All of which culminated in their being listed as an icon of England alongside Winston Churchill, Big Ben and the King James Bible.

The road Triumph roared down over the decades followed Britain's roller coaster twentieth century. The factory bore witness to political intrigue and betrayal before being saved from asset strippers by a worker's co-operative. Their obituary had been written time and again, but Mr Turner's motorcycle refused to die.

I spied the John O'Groats Hotel from the road, its Gothic spires unmistakable against the setting sun. Of all the places we had travelled in common, this was the one where his presence was most likely to be felt for the only changes were those wreaked by the passage of time and neglect.

I rode my motorcycle up to the front of the building, parking it where Mr Turner had parked his. I then took his old photograph out of my tank bag; we had arrived. The wind blew mercilessly across the empty car park, the sea was choppy and the skies heavy and leaden. For a moment it was just Mr Turner, myself and the wind whistling about the ramparts. I stretched my legs and looked out to the Isle of Stroma. Had he thought as I was thinking, that this is a desolate place?

In the photograph there were deck chairs and an old bench at the front of the building, but these were long gone. The name that had been proudly painted on the wall was still visible, but half a century of seawater and wind had taken its toll.

I held the photograph firmly as it shook in the north wind. There were shields on the side of the building. Once this place had been listed by the RAC, AA and Scottish Tourist Board and the owners proudly sported their seals of approval. These were old signs from a time that incorporated a regal inscription before the RAC and AA 'went corporate'. I strolled round the side of the building and sure enough there was the faded outline of the long gone signs, the rebrand having failed to reach this far north. Isolated cottages clung to the headland, their roofs low, bracing themselves against the relentless wind. I walked round the building as the vent in one of the upstairs windows rotated at full speed for the benefit of long departed guests. Had this place really ever had linen, room service and the choosy Mr Turner's patronage? It was hard to imagine.

"Arite ma friend?"

A young man, nine sheets to this particularly strong wind greeted me. His friend alighted from a battered car. He too liked a tipple as he made his way across the car park, limping for want of a pair of shoes. I noticed that he had a Celtic cum Rangers scar that stretched from his ear to the corner of his mouth that looked like his friend had stitched it during half time. I returned the greeting, walking the thin line between demonstrating that I did not want a fight on the one hand but on the other, neither did I want a conversation.

They left and it was just Mr Turner and me again. I positioned my motorcycle in exactly the same spot as had Mr Turner in the photograph and then placed my camera on a tripod some distance away. The car park certainly had not been resurfaced since 1953 and not only was I standing in the same location but in Mr Turner's footprints.

As I waited for the camera's timer I cast a glance over my shoulder. In my idle moments in the years leading up to this ride I had anticipated that at this point in time I would briefly catch a glimpse of an approving Mr Turner peering at me through the window. But the windows were whitewashed. And then the wind blew the tripod over which promptly triggered an upside down photograph of a car park badly in need of maintenance.

ENTER MR TURNER

Edward Turner (centre) with Alec Masters (left) and Robert Fearon (right)

Mr Turner was probably a genius. I do not mean that he had a crazy haircut and read too many books. His brand of genius was useful rather than incomprehensible. He was a doer rather than a talker and I suspect he never went on any management or gender awareness courses, for these were very different times.

Mr Turner was born on the night of Thursday the 24th of January, 1901 in Southwark, South London. Over the River Thames, King Edward VII acceded to the throne as Baby Edward Turner was accepted into a family of seven, a number necessitated by high infant mortality rates. Indeed his own life could have come to a very swift end when his nervous father dropped him at birth.

Bruises aside, Baby Edward was born into comparatively happy times. Whilst the lot of the working class was not great by modern standards, it was better than it had been under the Victorians. They were dying from fewer avoidable diseases, could vote, go to the Music Hall and occasionally take the train. Significantly, in a few years they would even have their own transport when bruised baby Edward from Southwark would come into his own.

The people from 'below stairs' were emerging to leave behind those conditioned only to serve their feudal masters, like Mundy the manservant in TH White's novel *Farewell Victoria*, who found his skills

> ...increasingly redundant ones in (his) later life. For after a spell in the Green Howards that included the bloody Zulu wars, he returned to a changing world. Gay King Edward made motoring fashionable; grooms and coachmen were a dying race. Mundy lived on, pathetically, in a world that had little place for him.

Soon a whole generation caught the whiff of petrol fumes down country lanes that had previously hummed with insects during the summertime and little else.

The past is not another country, it is another planet and Britons even spoke a different language. Self-belief shaped their every opinion and in an age before revisionist historians had to revise on pain of unemployment, there were a range of commonly held views that were unshakable. Into this world strode Mr Turner, as Baby Edward became known, carried along by his purposeful gait.

Mr Turner and his generation were amongst the last in a long lineage for whom adolescence and bayonets went together. For over a century, men of a certain age had found themselves stuffed uncomfortably into military uniform to engage in mortal struggle and button polishing. Mr Turner was not immune from these trappings despite the speculation that he was related to the 18th Century artist JMW Turner. Whatever his distant ancestors got up to, the current Turner family were engineers and Mr Turner was the best of them. His talents were first brought to the public's attention when the patrons of the local cinema were plunged into darkness. The cause had been Mr Turner's homemade welder in his father's neighbouring engineering works. He was a young man with little regard for the dimming of household lighting across the capital.

Those engineering talents left their mark on Nelson's Column, as his Lordship remains protected by four cast iron lions and some curious modern creations that largely go unnoticed. That he still stands there today is thanks to the Turner family business, for it was they who made the lightning conductor that runs its entire length. All of which left the Turner family modestly successful. And then came every parent's nightmare: a motorcycle. As a consequence Mr Turner experienced in quick succession, racing at Brooklands, a night in a police cell and a job in the motorcycle industry before acquiring a very pretty wife. It was 1929 and Mr Turner was twenty-eight. In the same way that today's bright young things go to the City to seek their fortunes, then they went to Coventry. Amazing but true.

A quarter of a century later Nelson remained gloriously strike free and about his feet was the rumbling of cars and the motorcycles that Mr Turner had designed, for by then Mr Turner was 'the boss' of Triumph motorcycles and no one dared to call him Edward.

In 'those days', as we call the past, cottage industries were almost the norm. A haphazard but enthusiastic network of individual businesses feeding everything from a war effort to an Empire. And Triumph motorcycles did all that in a changing world. The first signs of the biggest change was the emergence of that still deferential but increasingly mobile populace from 'below stairs'. Only mass production could meet their needs for which Triumph would need someone with vision, drive and the patronage of a super rich proprietor. Cometh the man, cometh the hour.

From 1936 Mr Turner stamped his mark on Triumph motorcycles and designed one of the milestones in motorcycle development: the Speed Twin. It was fast, cheap and caught the eye of every 'flash Harry' up and down the Kingdom. Mr Turner had brought to the masses the type of performance that WO Bentley could only provide in return for a blank cheque. Mr Turner had 'the knack' and kept it all his life. If the nation wanted speed, he gave it. If war intervened and they needed service, they got it. If austerity followed victory, so did Mr Turner, particularly in the Coronation year of 1953.

It was the start of a long hard road on which Mr Turner would build an icon fit for the coolest alpha males of several generations spanning Lee Marvin to Richard Gere. So satisfied was another customer called Bob Dylan that he wore his Triumph T-shirt on the cover of his best selling *Highway 61 Revisited* album; such a move would later be called 'product placement' by advertising executives. But for now, Bob just loved his motorcycle. And even the Queen gave her seal of approval by allowing Triumph to produce a limited edition to commemorate her silver jubilee. But in 1953 Mr Turner had no 'fancy ideas' over and above building the best motorcycle in the world.

Before the obsession with fashion, Britain lived in austere and functional times and motorcycles sold on economy and reliability. To demonstrate both Mr Turner selected his smallest model from the production line and proposed to ride it from Land's End to John O'Groats. He would ride a motorcycle designed by him, made in a factory run by him over 1,008 miles. Thus on Monday the 5th of October, 1953 the doorman promptly opened the gates of the Triumph offices in Meriden, Warwickshire: the place, which Mr Turner always called his 'little factory in England'. Three riders immaculately clad in brand new Barbour suits emerged from under the huge Triumph sign and gently fluttering Union Jack that always flew from the factory's flagpole. Three smart new Triumph Terrier motorcycles awaited Mr Turner, managing director, Robert Fearon, works director and Alec St John Masters, chief designer. Behind them was Colin Swaisland, a cameraman from ESSO Petroleum on a larger 500cc Speed Twin, Mr Turner's long suffering driver, Frank Griffith behind the wheel of a Sunbeam-Talbot motorcar and the ACU's official observer John McNulty who shared the driving of the factory estate car with Triumph's Eric Headlam.

The sweep round drive that bordered Triumph's finely manicured lawns led to two wrought iron gates. They sport the logo of the best motorcycle in the world.

When this particular factory finally closed in 1983, a former Triumph draughtsman moved in and bought them for his business premises with a speed that befits the world speed record holder that he is. They still hang today at Norman Hyde Enterprises Limited and they were one of a number of all-British sponsors of my subsequent recreation of Mr Turner's ride.

All three riders had been weighed, the oil and petrol levels had been checked in the presence of observer McNulty. It would be the last time Mr Turner would see the factory to which he had devoted his life and talents for a full week. The engines were started and moments later the convoy swept through Triumph's famous gates and headed due south. The Gaffer's Gallop had begun.

MEANWHILE...

My own fanfare and departure was a little less dramatic than Mr Turner's. For a start all this was the wrong way round and I simply did not want to go. Whilst my trips across Europe had been a little grander, they fell well short of the man making rights of passage trips across burning deserts. And to show that I had completely misunderstood Jack Kerouac's novel On The Road, I decided to get qualified and mortgaged before doing the 'road trip' thing again. On that road, I told Tilly, my wife, you just have to let things happen, as things do just happen. And so I persuaded her to take a honeymoon, 'on the road', on a Triumph and perhaps least agreeable of all, with me. But for various reasons I was making this particular trip alone.

I was still reluctant to go and for the last week the media had dished out a never-ending diet of 'only travel if you have to' headlines. For once they had good reason; the nation was flooded, people were being washed away and in that uniquely British fashion, rescuing the incumbents of the dog's home was considered newsworthy. I drew back the curtains at dawn to see that the rain was at forty-five degrees and clearly intended to stay that way. Outside and getting wet was my very own 1995 Triumph Thunderbird 900.

Mr Turner's bike weighed half as much as mine and had one cylinder, one carburettor and would return over a hundred miles to the gallon. I have three cylinders, a bank of carburettors and as many valves as a Jaguar racing car of 1953 vintage. I do not particularly want them but I do end up with fifty-brake horsepower more than Mr Turner. Of one thing there is no doubt, I will be far more comfortable than he ever was.

Comfortable or not I still do not want to go and probably would not but for feeling obliged to my chosen charity and my sponsors, not least UKBIKER who had built me a spiffing website that announced to the world that today was the day.

Since I have been planning this ride I have also acquired a son, Benedict who watches me from his high chair as I walk grumpily passed with my luggage and an assortment of bungees. He is seven months old and so cannot possibly call out "Daddy don't go", but I am sure he does. And the cosy kitchen smells of fresh ground coffee, even though there isn't any on the go, and if I walked passed the empty fireplace I am sure I would see flames licking up the chimney. In short there's a big red neon sign above the house reading, 'Don't go ya jackass'.

I'm in good company. John Steinbeck acquired the Nobel Prize with these lines from *Travels With Charlie*:-

In long range planning for a trip, I think there is a private conviction that it won't happen. As the day approached, my warm bed and comfortable house grew increasingly desirable and my dear wife incalculably precious.

And still it rained. A puddle had formed around the side stand and I was worried that my sponsor's stickers may not see it through the first day. I had similar worries about the rider.

A little later than expected I undertook the arduous task of dressing myself in a fashion that would keep me dry for six hours under a power hose. Like Mr Turner I wore a brand new Barbour jacket. It was identical in every respect to his and has been in continuous production for over half a century. Submariners originally wore them during the Second World War and it's sealed collars and cuffs subsequently proved ideal for motorcycling. Right up until the eighties Barbour jackets set the standard against which all motorcycle jackets were judged. They were for the 'serious motorcyclist' and worn by my Dad and all his mates. However with the passing years 'noddy suits' seem to have become many motorcyclists' preferred haute couture. I duly telephoned Barbour some weeks before my departure and a charming but nervous lady told me that they lacked the noddy body armour that would at least make me look broad shouldered if nothing else. I suspect that she also feared being sued, which is a little ironic given that I was escaping from my job as a litigation lawyer for a week. Finally I threw my leg over the bike, cast a last glance up the drive to see Tilly recording my departure on a camcorder and left with a lump in my throat. It isn't very butch I confess, but there you have it.

Within a hundred yards one of the two Cancer Research flags I'd bungeed to the back of the bike broke free and spent the rest of the week in the gutter around the corner from our house, but I was on my way. The rain couldn't touch me, the road unfolded and the lump in my throat rapidly subsided. Within fifty miles my remaining Cancer Research flag had turned to a papier-mâché pulp and was plastered across my luggage. It was not an omen, for I was as happy as the proverbial pig in manure and stayed that way for the rest of the week. It was still the early morning and the roads were empty. I had supreme confidence in the bike to which I had strapped everything I needed for the next 2,000 miles. And that is as good as life gets.

THE ILLUSIVE JERUSALEM

On a 'road trip', the fun starts the moment the front door closes, or so says many a biker down the pub with or without first hand knowledge. It was nearly like that for Mr Turner but his ride was a publicity stunt: working, if not at the office. The photograph at the end of the ride shows a grinning Mr Turner with a carefree demeanour and that's a pretty good advert for the open road, particularly to those who knew him.

Having swept through the factory gates the convoy straightened up, wound back their throttles and headed south. The factory diminished in the Sunbeam's rear view mirror, if not so swiftly in Mr Turner's mind.

In 1953 Britain had the British disease. Peter Sellers had the British disease in the Ealing Comedy *I'm Alright Jack*, which was all about our penchant for strikes. They were as much a part of the English social calendar as Henley and Ascot and they rolled off the production line at a rate that impressed even the Japanese and Germans. We produced the most powerful, durable and reliable strikes of any industrial nation and in this chosen field were truly great once more.

Strikes also affected the motorcycle industry and in Triumph there was a comparatively high number of happy motorcyclists amongst the work force. Just as well; Mr Turner was no diplomat and yet even this could work to his advantage. Thus when the unions in the chrome-plating department failed to produce petrol tanks to his high standards he raged:-

As of today no further petrol tanks will be made at Triumph because it's a menace. From now on we shall stove enamel our tanks and we shall design a motif to provide the glitter.

Meanwhile Mr Turner and his convoy wound their way through Shakespeare country on 'A' roads that bowed to the rivers and hills. In the Indian summer of 1953 the sun reflected in the river Avon and the willow trees hung over the water's surface in the motionless autumn air. He could have stolen himself a sentimental moment to believe that this was indeed that 'Other Eden…this blessed spot…this England' and all that. And had he done so, all in earshot would probably have agreed, for this was the era before cuddly liberals beat themselves up over imperial pith helmets popping up across the globe. Instead the antics of bully boy shop stewards were the forerunner of political correctness giving them the right to address a Minister of State as 'brother and comrade' at the height of the cold war. Crazy days.

Any sane motorcyclist would have put such woes behind him and no better tonic than the rush of wind on the open road for that, and no better road than the Roman Fosse Way. Straight as a dart from Lincoln to Exeter which then enjoyed the remote feel that only 1953's weight of traffic could bestow upon it.

Despite the era Mr Turner himself had an enviable record with his staff. Surprisingly, one would have to search hard to find evidence of him ever sacking anyone in all his years at Triumph. His driver, Frank Griffith, invariably came in for the worst treatment and they spent decades thrusting at each other with letters of resignation and dismissal like exhausted knights not knowing when to stop jousting in a bad *Monty Python* sketch. But this was no Baldric and Blackadder relationship, for there was a time in Mr Turner's life when he desperately needed Frank to be there when tragedy struck.

Then as now the traveller along the Fosse Way passed through innumerable parish and county boundaries from St George The Martyr in Exeter to St Peter At Gowts in Lincoln. Mr Turner's convoy interrupted the peace of the villages along the roadside with their church spires, sighing copses and British Legion Clubs. Most of the village greens were illuminated by the lamplight, revealing stone memorials to the fallen which bore the names of those who made the ultimate sacrifice simply because it was expected of them. They gave it all on the promise of a New Jerusalem that never came. After living amidst the ruins of a war torn Europe, the survivors came home to a war torn Britain, rationing, snow and the first banana boat for six years. Officers in trilbies managed post war Britain and the ranks in caps still were expected to do as they were told. They found it difficult to risk their lives one day and then go back to the shipyard gates, cap in hand the next. And why should they? For the rest of the century Britain was run on a 'them and us' basis. It did not work then and it probably did not work when the Romans passed this way either.

ON THE ROAD AGAIN

One of the things I have learnt from my time 'on the road'; an expression I use all too readily to describe a mere holiday, is that it is a good thing to get up early in the morning. Had I continued riding into the sunset I might have discovered something more profound. Still, better a modest lesson than no lesson at all.

The previous evening I had studied the weather forecast and concluded that hypothermia can come around remarkably quickly. That's why I chose to forsake paisley patterned bandanas and sunglasses for big boots and gauntlets. It has to be said that I cut a particularly neat dash in a waterproof kind of way.

And so the road unfolded, winding its way west in the early morning drizzle. Minor roads that defer to hedgerows, the towns decreasing in size and the countryside opening out. Slowly humanity was emerging as I rode by, unnoticed in their everyday lives. Sensible chaps in slacks came strolling down the road from the corner shop with their Sunday papers and cars poked their bonnets out of side roads where half an hour earlier there had been none.

The benefit of getting up early reveals itself in the form of landmarks that flash by before breakfast that would normally be a day trip away. With the drizzle now turning to rain and stalking me across Salisbury Plain I happen upon an anonymous pile of rubble uncomfortably sandwiched between two main roads. Perhaps this is why someone has carved into the wall of the stylish public lavatories at Stonehenge 'I can't believe that I've travelled 6,000 miles just to see this'.

Leaving the graffiti behind I have the open road ahead of me as Dorset becomes Devon and Devon becomes Cornwall. The cloud breaks up and I catch my first glimpse of the sea as I ride past St Michaels Mount where the waves gently flop on the shore, falter and retire. On reaching Land's End I fill out the visitor's book in the hotel foyer and note the names of those who have completed what I am about to begin.

"I think you'll find the facilities down here are better," advises the kindly concierge as he takes my photograph on the very spot where Mr Turner once stood.

That evening I stroll to the Logan Rock and stand on the cliff top in complete silence, except for the distant whisper of the sea at their feet below. After a pint of St Austell in the nearest pub I retire to a deep sleep, disturbed only by the occasional gust of wind straight off the sea.

THE FERTILISATION CEREMONY

On the evening of Monday the 5th of October 1953 the nation went home to its fireside, tuned in the 'wireless' and settled down to the soothing tones of men with reassuringly solid sounding names like Wyndham Milligan and Guy Kingsley Poynter who gathered around a microphone in Shepherd's Bush. From here their voices were beamed across the Kingdom and reached homes as far west as Exeter.

As Mr Turner's convoy approached that ancient city the riders were struck by the beautiful sunset. They were making their way down the lower leg of Britain and into the mystical south-west. Once the sun went down and the few petrol stations closed at 5 pm prompt, you were in for the night.

Two years earlier, Festival of Britain fever had gripped Exeter and the war damage was being put right. Sentiment about architecture was nearly two decades away and Exeter was just plain old. Consequently, the High Street had been rebuilt and road widening had been necessitated by the growing use of the motorcar. In 1953 there were nearly three million of them. Even so the convoy's gentle glide through Exeter at the end of a long day was largely unhindered.

The lights were going out across the town centre. Cornish's gentleman's outfitters had sold their last cravat for the day and Smith's grocers had no need to worry about the competition from Tescos: the first supermarket did not arrive in the town until 1958. When the doors were bolted, staff and management alike walked to the bus stop, confident in the knowledge that their jobs would still be there in the morning.

Mr Turner would not for one moment have been sentimental about the changes which he would see as necessary to keep the nation competitive. And his path was made easier by the absence of Exeter's once famous trams, by then another victim of progress having been consigned to a field out of town.

Perhaps the office girls, bank managers, window cleaners and war heroes who watched the convoy rumble gently by were envious as they stood in the bus queue. Perhaps not, for this was the age when you were supposed to 'accept your lot'.

All afternoon the old bus station in Paul Street had prepared for the rush hour when its entire complement of thirteen Daimler buses would be responsible for getting Exeter safely home. After Mr Turner had passed, the commuters would catch their first glimpse of the familiar cream and green livery of their friendly local bus as it rounded the corner.

Meanwhile the convoy headed for St David's Hill, not far from the railway station. At the foot of the hill was the gated entrance to that stately pile known as the Imperial Hotel. The Commander of The Bath who had previously lived there never thought that motorcyclists would crunch his gravel drive but the current incumbents, Witherspoons, might cause his monocle to drop in his soup.

From the magnificent Orangery the staff could see the four motorcycle headlights cutting their way through the gathering darkness. Not many motorcyclists could afford the one pound a night tariff and the staff could tell by the mannerisms of those around Mr Turner that he was in charge. His jokes were laughed at and could be heard throughout the building as the lights burned brightly into the night. Outside, Exeter had fallen quiet. Occasionally people emerged from pubs and went on their way as the city ran it's skeleton night time bus service. Those feeling 'flush' went to the Odeon cinema on Sidwell Street and watched the sheriff keep order in some frontier town. Outside the street lights burned, but far from brightly and the stars could be clearly seen. Sports bars, fruit machines and juke boxes were at least a decade away and the only sound was distant laughter that intensified as the pub doors occasionally swung open to reveal their smoky world.

It is not difficult for the generation that shared these tranquil nights in the 1950s to grow sentimental about them. There was no litter simply because the nation could not afford to wrap everything in plastic. The crime rate seemed lower because people were listening to that 'wireless' rather than watching *Crime Watch*. If there was a scream or smashing of plates next door then you learned to pretend you had not heard it. Minding your own business was a virtue and the crime figures never went behind a man's own front door. And behind many a door came drink soaked questions about what really went on during the war while they were away. One way or another the sentiments of Robert Douglas in *Night Song Of The Last Tram* were more common than many care to remember when he wrote:-

> *If my father, Robert John Douglas, had been killed in North Africa or Italy during the Second World War, I know that for the rest of my life I would have looked at photographs of him and mourned our lost relationship. Unfortunately, he survived and came home.*

At the foot of St David's was the railway station from where the ghostly whistle of the night train could be heard before evaporating with the steam. Moored in the Exeter canal was the vessel *Wolanda* from whose cast iron hull stevedores had unloaded timber and oil. Now the moonlight reflected in the water that was as still as a millpond and the only connection with the outside world were those good men of the BBC in faraway Shepherd's Bush.

If the staff of the Imperial Hotel hoped to clock off early then they would be disappointed. Mr Turner kept them busy into the night for he was on form. Over two hundred miles of fresh air had done him good, particularly after he thought that the Gaffers' Gallop would come to an ignominious end following one Gaffer's disappearance in a cloud of smoke. This turned out to be powdered fertilizer dropped by a passing truck and jokes about the fertilization ceremony abounded into the night.

In the town, the cinemagoers tried to crush onto the last bus. Those that failed faced another long walk home. And then the town fell silent, except for the bells of Exeter Cathedral and Mr Turner.

COOL CAMPING

The following morning brought brilliant sunshine, albeit above a thick blanket of cloud. In the early hours I had been reminded of how incredibly loud rain on canvas can be. Having dared venture out during a break in the weather, I spied a red line that was the sunrise on the distant horizon.

On a bench between two camper vans of snoring surfers I penned a postcard home before strolling down the track to the postbox. The hedges were heavy with the damp as the sun came up and cast an almost violet hue under the ceiling of cloud. I dropped my cards in the postbox and then packed the Triumph that had spent a cosy night in the farmer's barn.

With the aid of enough bungees to jump off the cliffs, I strapped my bags to the Triumph only to be joined by the farmer who, like pragmatic rural folk everywhere, did what he needed to survive and set up a campsite: people pay better than livestock.

We chatted briefly and like most Cornishmen he welcomed wealthy Londoners who spent their money in his county. I was touchier about this, probably because I'm not wealthy and perhaps because of the number of television programmes encouraging sentimental town dwellers to relocate to the country to make a living out of growing organic mushrooms or something equally implausible. "Aah them. We see them come and we see them go," he said reflectively. And with that I started the Triumph and left myself.

HEIYO MARU

Mr Turner slept soundly through the first anniversary of one of the most significant events of the twentieth century. It was exactly one year to the very day since the Japanese freighter, the *Heiyo Maru,* left Tilbury docks and set in motion events that would shape the second half of the century. Her passenger list read like the cast of an Agatha Christie thriller; a British diplomat and his Danish wife, a British woman en route to joining an American army officer and finally a secretive Australian. This gives little clue to the significance of this sixteen thousand ton vessel, the very first on the high seas since Japan's defeat. Long after the passengers had disembarked at Kobe, forty-nine days later, the anonymous sacks of concrete came ashore, along with a consignment of a car the British considered a joke, the Volkswagen Beetle. Japan had no car industry and a lot of building work to complete. These were her very first steps to becoming an economic superpower and ultimately the world's biggest producer of motorcycles.

The following morning the Gaffers joined the county set in the Imperial's dining hall. Like well-dressed motorcyclists the world over they were collared and tied underneath their tweeds as Mr Turner held court over full English breakfast. Waiters came and during a lull in the conversation Mr Turner could pick out the headlines. While the Imperial had resonated to the snoring of three middle-aged motorcyclists, a gunboat had slipped out of harbour under cover of darkness bound for British Guiana. Whatever the problem was, the solution would make up for its shortcomings in subtlety with an abundance of effectiveness, or so contemporary thinking went.

Churchill was still in power and like so many of his generation, Mr Turner framed himself upon the octogenarian Prime Minister and to all intents and purposes affected a Churchillian stature. In the way that Churchill kept senior civil servants running down Whitehall corridors and was contemptuous of red tape, Mr Turner carried that same impatience into a motorcycle factory. For better or worse, it was the twilight of the no nonsense school of leadership.

Booted and Barboured the Gaffers strolled out through the Imperial's ornate ivy clad entrance and into the morning sun. "This is just the job – I needed this to jerk me out of a groove", exclaimed Mr Turner to the special correspondent from *MotorCycling* magazine.

The motorcycles were started and the convoy rumbled out. That same correspondent noted that all three Gaffers kept perfect formation and their passing could be heard by the ladies of the parish who were preparing the alter flowers in Exeter Cathedral. However they were more concerned by the theft of the alter cross. This was Exeter, a place of worship and the dawn of a new Elizabethan age. They concluded that the theft was a temporary aberration and nothing to do with the stout yeoman of Devon. Blame was instantly placed at the foot of a 'London gang', particularly when a stolen get-away car was found pointing in the direction of the capital. They concluded that the real problem was the sudden freedom of private transport thrust upon those who were not used to it. No longer could a paternal, but unquestionably superior squire mete out summary justice backed up by the strong arm of his gamekeeper; soon they will all be out of reach.

HURRICANES AND WINDMILLS

Whenever Hurricane Brenda hit Alabama, or some other exotic clime ,the news footage would invariably show a wildly swaying palm tree. It was therefore such a disappointment to find that the one on the roundabout outside a shopping centre in Penzance looked suspiciously like the one the cash strapped BBC play each time they report on a natural disaster.

Flaming June or not it was still raining. The wind blew through deserted villages with abandoned tin mines and half-eaten cream teas. In the middle of the day it became so dark that the street lights came on, at which point most normal people would probably have wished they had gone to Benidorm instead.

The swell from my tracks splayed out across the flooded road; a depressing spectacle if you had booked a week's holiday here. I may be riding a motorcycle in what looks like a trawler man's outfit but at least I can ride out of town and, had there been one, into the sunset. The locals looked at me as if I was the unfortunate one, but I was in fact enjoying myself, as was DH Lawrence when he wrote:-

> Cornwall is very primeval; great, black, jutting cliffs and rocks and a pale
> of sea breaking in, it is like the very beginning of the world, wonderful: and
> so free and strong.

But I knew not what Lawrence would have made of the modest watering hole of 1649 vintage, known as The Victoria Inn at Roche. Alas Lawrence, were he moved to poetry would not have had to wrack his brain for words to rhyme with 'ample parking' or 'conference facilities'. In his day it was just a solid stone cottage by the road selling beer, whereas to me it was a place of great history; worthy of a blue plaque. It drifted into my imagination as a place that had not changed since 1953. There was no need for it to change from the old photograph with French shutters and the archway through which Mr Turner had once passed. In my idle moments in the office I had often pulled out the road atlas from the bottom draw of my desk. Even on a map it looked anonymous. I imagined strolling into the bar, seating myself by the fireside and opening with the purpose of my journey. Perhaps there would be some old toper who could remember the day, many years ago, when three mysterious motorcyclists rode into town.

THE VICTORIA INN

To the Gaffers, The Victoria Inn was a place to see an old friend, Alan Maclachlan (Winco Mac), who had left behind the turmoil of commercial life to run a country pub. The Terriers were off with Colin Swaisland and his camera on the Speed Twin following with Triumph's customary roar as the cars brought up the rear.

Winco wiped down the bar and awaited the arrival of three old friends. He was looking forward to it. He was a 'petrol head' and there weren't many of those in a small community of 6,000 acres and 1,865 farm hands. Winco was also one of the founding fathers of amateur motor sport. In his day the sheds and back gardens of Britain would occasionally resonate to tiny but highly tuned engines prepared by amateurs in tank tops with spanners. And under the empty skies of the Sussex Downs they were put to the test at the Lewes Hill Climb. Homemade cars roared up the chalk slopes as the skylarks ascended nervously above the fray. Men in tweeds, without helmets, wrestled with the steering as spoked wheels threw out dust on sharp corners. Malcolm Campbell was amongst their number in the days before fame and knighthood came his way and, like Winco Mac, he just got on with it. Impromptu, amateur and possibly a little dangerous, it was undeniably happy, but it couldn't last. Its life span was a couple of years and the few remaining photographs bear witness to their carefree faces succumbing to the shadow of a pensive expression as the thirties drew to a close. A number would shortly be flung to all the corners of the globe to defend their own freedom and that of the world. Unlike the skylarks, they never came back.

After the war, the nation was charged to export or die. Brooklands' banked track fell to weeds, rationing limited motor sport and Winco became head of the RAC motorcycle section where he met, did business and became firm friends with Mr Turner.

Winco heard the unmistakable exhaust note of Triumph motorcycles coming down the road. By the time he had unbolted the door, three Terriers were pulling up outside and the Inn promptly filled with greeting and good cheer. The article that appeared in *MotorCycling* magazine the following week records:-

> *Today's start, incidentally, was from the Victoria Inn at Roche, near Bodmin, where former RAC motorcycle department manager, Alan Maclachlan ('Winco Mac') and his charming wife were found to be in fine form.*

It omitted to mention the chill we all feel when somebody walks over our grave. Bob Fearon swivelled round on his bar stool and looked through the entrance and into the car park.

"Whose that queer looking character photographing your pub sign, Winco?"

"He's not one of the locals that's for sure."

Mr Turner lowered his glass and looked up.

"I wonder where his bike is?"

"Looks like that one over there," said Alec St John Masters.

Mr Turner went to the side window facing the main road.

"Come and look at this."

Alec and Bob cast each other a glance and then joined Mr Turner.

"Good grief", they exclaimed in unison, "look at the quality of the engineering."

"That I will grant you," said Mr Turner, "but I'm not convinced a motorcycle should be so top heavy, and look at the thickness of that back tyre. It lacks the simplicity and fine balance of a Speed Twin. And there's too much chrome; that'll cost a fortune."

Alec looked to the left, "Here he comes now."

"No kick start, now that's a development," noted Mr Turner.

"If only we could see the name on the tank".

But he was gone.

THE VICTORIA INN REVISITED

The idea of recreating the Gaffers' Gallop came to me three years earlier when I worked for a law firm specialising in suing drivers who had knocked over my brethren bikers (it was never the other way around). I put in a mass of effort with a view to raising a fortune for charity, but still the press and public alike failed to treat me as the visionary fundraiser that I am, so I just had a good time all the same. During the preceding years I had plenty of opportunity to map out my journey in my mind's eye. Of course *Halsbury's Statutes Of England* surrounded me and I prepared writs and appeals a plenty, assisting any court seized of my litigation, as you do. But as soon as the verdict was reached, my thoughts all too easily drifted to the open road as I played out an imaginary ciné reel of long fast bends. I knew Mr Turner's route by heart and those places that he stopped at acquired a mythical status. The first was The Victoria Inn at Roche in Cornwall. As with modern motorcycles on modern roads my destination came around with alarming speed, but before paying homage I pulled into the village petrol station to top up. The wind blew the flags at the neighbouring caravan shop, the adjacent transport café was empty and its car park full of potholes and puddles. The main road had passed through here in Mr Turner's day but the dual carriageway had since taken away its lifeblood. It now existed for what was left behind; not much.

I paid for the petrol and rode out of the petrol station reverentially. The locals may have thought 'There goes a queer looking fellow so tightly wrapped in waterproofs he looks like a Michelin man on a motorbike. And the really weird thing is that he is photographing the swaying sign of The Victoria Inn'. But instead they all chose to stay indoors leaving me alone to see the sights. The pine showroom opposite was closed and a scattering of vehicles in the used car lot had no punters. Not quite the rural retreat into which Winco Mac became happily ensconced.

Our collective efforts sweep away the past on a daily basis. Our roads straighten, widen and increase the speed and flow of the traffic and by pass pleasure for purpose. Yet in quiet corners of the old country there is still the occasional red phone box or ancient church spire that airily gazes down on the chaos below. However, in architecture the British have singularly failed to grasp the notion of evolution. To many, what the Luftwaffe started, the architects and town planners completed, except at The Victoria Inn. That archway through which Mr Turner had passed was still there, contained within a modern conservatory. The continental shutters now faced out over the Inn's extensive car park. 'Bob 'n' Betty' promise to give everyone a warm welcome, according to the website, and there are forty-two extra rooms available in the extension to the rear of the original building. Today's only links with petrol are the regular meetings of local trial riders whose muddy presence Mr Turner would doubtless approve of.

Whilst buildings up and down the country bear blue plaques by virtue of having some association with luminaries such as William Wordsworth, Michael Faraday and erm… Frankie Howerd, there is no blue plaque at The Victoria Inn for Mr Turner.

I peered in through the utterly empty entrance clocking the red carpet, dark wood reception and courtesy light, which gave the place a welcoming, glow. Bob 'n' Betty were not around and neither were their customers. There were no old topers at the bar but the car park was full of reps cars. Once, three Triumph Terriers graced the front of the building before the conservatory and conference facilities or even the birth of either Bob or Betty.

Another squall of showers swept across the car park and awoke me from 1953. There was nothing here at all and I had many miles ahead of me and an uncertain night stop. I walked round to the side of the building where the side window was adjacent to the main road where I had parked the bike. I threw my leg over the laden Thunderbird, pressed the starter and throttled off to the neighbouring parish of St Wenn and Withiel; now you don't get names like that in a Jack Kerouac novel!

RETURN TO THE IMPERIAL

The drawing rooms of England are dangerous places. Their oak panels, eternally roaring fires and deep leather sofas have provided a secure cocoon for generals, politicians and captains of industry regardless of merit. Whatever was happening in the trenches and on the factory floors, 'there'll always be an England' as the song goes. We have London clubs, Royal barracks, Volkswagen powered Bentleys and little to export, yet the drawing rooms feel the same today as they did in 1953. In the half century since, their oak panelled walls held back the cold wind of reality. Then it was merely a draught by comparison to what was to come. Seven years after the Gaffers' Gallop Mr Turner prophesied an industrial hurricane, and he was right even if he had never heard of the *Heiyo Maru*.

From the drawing room of the Imperial, Mr Turner reflected on the first day of the Gallop. Oak panelled walls never managed to sever him from reality and he was after all parading before a hungry nation his 'poor man's motorcycle'.

The three Terriers had tackled their task with 'jaunt and verve' as ESSO's cameraman moved fore and aft the Gaffers to get the best shots. Mr Turner was blasé instructing Swaisland to "nip ahead now and then old boy" to do a bit of shooting. "This was a well drilled team," reported *MotorCycling* magazine a week later and that the scheduled average speed of 30 mph turned out to be 38.

The official observation for the Gallop had started at The Victoria Inn from where the Gaffers rode to Land's End. 'The promise of yesterday's sunset was amply fulfilled and Land's End was at its best' reported the magazine. On returning to the Imperial all riders were in the best of spirits. The night drew in and the portraits of the great and good in the drawing rooms of the nation looked down imperiously on those charged with shaping the future. Churchill was in Downing Street; Eisenhower was in the Whitehouse with McCarthy at the movies whilst Stalin had departed for the great Vodka factory in the sky.

Mr Turner could sink back into his big leather armchair as he had his nightcap and reflect on the past and the uncertain future. Four months earlier Churchill had a massive stroke and his legend, which hadn't yet been established, would be based on his wartime leadership. The end was coming, but not before the grand old man came out into the ring for a stellar performance during the same week as the Gaffer's Gallop. Speaking in Margate and on his feet for fifty minutes, without trace of frailty, he addressed the issue of the unions whom he felt had an 'important part' to play in British life:-

> Restraining the featherheads, crackpots, vote catchers and office seekers from putting the folly they talk into action.

These words were noted in the drawing rooms across the nation.

Nightcap over, Mr Turner may well have taken that week's copy of *MotorCycling* to bed to read of Britain's victory in the International Six Day Trial and the part played by Jim Alves on a Triumph 650. At page 13 he could read the advert titled 'thoroughbred through and through' that concluded with the words, 'Triumph, The Best Motorcycle In The World'. He could sleep well.

MALCOLM'S PIANO

BBC radio was warning commuters in Kent of traffic jams on the M25 while I had the A30 over Bodmin Moor to myself. Up here it is a practical existence and even the trees accept the inevitable and bow to the climate by growing at an angle. On the moor the farmers are frequently called out in storms at midnight to their flocks and if they take much notice of the health and safety laws they probably do not stay in business for long.

Onward and upward passed Dozmary Pool where the 'Lady Of The Lake' handed over King Arthur's Excalibur (according to the tourist board) and a church where the vicar compensated for his dwindling flock by putting cardboard cut-outs on the pews (according to his bemused parishioners). All this culminated in that peak known as Brown Willy but on this day Willy was hidden by the never ending stair rods.

Down the Moor and I enter the city of Exeter about which Sir John Betjeman wrote of the typical visitor that:-

> *He will lose his temper with the appalling jam of traffic which there always seems to be in Exeter High Street – I hope to goodness they'll get a new bypass or two finished soon…*

Lines first broadcast in 1937 still have a resonance today as I was corralled onto that bypass only to be ushered from one roundabout to the next. The traffic was still jammed and I was in the fast lane facing north. I was then herded away from the town when I wanted to be in the centre and on my way to Mr Turner's Imperial Hotel. I found another roundabout and rode around it half a dozen times trying to read all the road signs at my leisure. This probably was not what the town planner intended but I had no intention of being sucked around a town at one end, only to be spat out at the other; this was personal. Finally I broke the curse and turned off the bypass and entered an historic town previously hidden by signs that read 'Exeter – Historic Town'.

Embarrassed at my inability to find a hotel on a hill in a provincial English town, which bodes ill for reaching the other side of the Kingdom, I persevere. Then I round the foot of a wooded hill and am stopped smartly by a 'road blocked' sign. The wind has brought down several trees whose trunks lie across the road whilst legions of chaps in Hi-Viz jackets are safely visible as they scratch their chins. Beyond them lies the Imperial Hotel and I finally decide to lop off historical integrity and head out of town.

You are never in for the night in Exeter anymore and seldom do you see the stars above the neon glare. Three lane carriageways take you up to the traffic lights on the road out of town heading east. A flyover provides temporary respite from the weather as articulated lorries rumble to a standstill alongside, carrying the canal's cargo for today's impatient world. The tail fins of commercial aeroplanes line the embankment as one after another take to the air and are rapidly engulfed by the low cloud. Forgotten in a field under their flight path are the remains of Exeter's trams.

Reigning in my sentiment, I recall one Victorian pub I passed on my tour of the town's arterial roads. Unspoilt and with chalk boards boasting real ale, I pen in my mind's eye a slap across the face for those modern architects who think that townscapes should look like the junk monster has regurgitated his supper. You are spared this by the dark reality of what actually went on inside those four walls, as the board outside read:-

SATURDAY IS 60S NIGHT,
SUNDAY DISCO NIGHT,
MONDAY WITH MALCOLM ON THE PIANO

I avoid Malcolm and follow the tyre tracks of those villains from the Cathedral and head out towards Honiton on the A30 through the Vale of Teleford. This is everyone's introduction to the South West as they witness the unfolding countryside and the idiosyncrasies of a landscape shaped by the local economy in a far slower gear than elsewhere. For the time being at least, holidaymakers can relish a journey through avenues of trees and remarkably, some roads with bends!

Arriving in Honiton I seek out a petrol station, as regular stops are the price you pay for a big engine and a small, if remarkably handsome, petrol tank. I have doubts about actually completing this journey as I take a photograph of the bike alongside a headline on the *Daily Express* newsstand, which read, 'Today Is The Wettest Day For 50 Years'. It was a relief: I was beginning to wonder if it was me.

Inside the petrol station people picked up their papers, chatted to their neighbours and I suspected they all had a pretty good idea where they would be sleeping that night. In most cases they did not doubt that they would be warm and dry. They had no idea how lucky they were.

Devon gave way to Wiltshire and then Somerset as I clocked up the miles; the rain eased up and I passed through a string of sleepy villages. Then I noticed something. I was off the beaten track, on narrow winding lanes with hedgerows holding back fields of swaying barley. Again I noticed it: a dry patch on the road. And another. Heavy as the clouds may be, the mid-afternoon was quiet and people were emerging from their cottages to peer up at the sky. Someone thought they had spotted sunshine!

The names of the villages were pure wacky south west, Shepton Beauchamp, Beecham Weston, Compton Pauncefoot, but I was to settle for Bowdens Crest and my campsite. I meandered up an ever-narrowing road with grass growing in the middle till I reached a ridge and a fifty's wooden fingerpost road sign. I turned left and followed the ridge overlooking the Somerset levels. Hidden off the road behind electric gates was my campsite for the night. I passed through the entrance which looked like it had been decorated with the contents of a garden centre and rode into a field in which caravans were arranged in a circle around the perimeter. In the middle were three tall silver birch trees forming a triangle, the middle of which was to be my home for the night. It isn't so long since such places bristled with 'No Bikers' signs and so when the old dame in charge emerged from her static caravan, I felt like ingratiating on pain of a night in 'ye olde draftee bus shelter'.

"You're supposed to stop at the gate."

"Sorry…"

"It's five pounds a night and the gates close at ten pm and they don't open till seven am."

"Suits me, that will keep the ruffians out."

I duly paid, which pleased her and watched her pad off in her slippers. I was, it appeared the only camper and for some time thought that I was going to be alone with Mrs Slippers for the night.

Once my tent was up I felt at home and strolled around the ridge. The trees had been cleared allowing a spectacular view of the Quantocks under the leaden sky. The sun was going down and in the vale the floodwaters were coming up. As a consequence all the roads were impassable and in the distance workmen were doing repairs through the night. I could see a flashing light and occasionally a reverse warning tone drifted along over the silence. With or without those electric gates, we were in for the night.

The lights came on in the log cabin and a grand total of six of us sat under the pine roof drinking Somerset cider. Mrs Slippers' daughter served at the bar and her jockey sized husband kept a pair of hairy Brummies in conversation.

"Amazin' in't eet?" said Mr Brum from under his Viking warlord 'hairdo'. Quite what was amazing I did not know, but fancied it was a general comment about life rather than the lack of customers and so concurred. His wife sat uncomfortably either side of one stool when she really needed three. Picking at her bowl of chips she ran through the times they had stayed at the site.

"You didn't have the cabin then did you?"

"No", replied the jockey who turned out to be Irish.

"We bought ours in Wales after we'd seen yours."

"You did, so you did."

"That was after we'd been to Kathmandu."

"It was, so it was."

"Did we ever tell you about Kathmandu?"

"Aaah, you did that, a time a two I believe."

"And the wooden elephants we brought back?"

"To be sure."

She looked disappointed.

"But oil bet tha's something ya missed out so ya can tell me again if yer like."

And she did, so she did.

The night drew in and I finished my cider and repaired to my canvas home under the silver birches swaying in the night breeze. Boots off and tent zipped up, the only sound was the road works in the vale and the dying embers of the Glastonbury Festival in the distance. I was not counting sheep for long.

THE WILD ONE

When the clapper board snapped shut for the last time heralding the final out take of *The Wild One*, it set in motion the greatest free commercial for a brand in history; and it was Triumphs. The first iconic stills of a moody Marlon Brando leaning between the high bars of his Triumph Thunderbird were not the image that Triumph were looking for in 1953.

Filmed at the same time as the Gaffers' Gallop, the movie was immediately banned in the UK which only added to its kudos. This was the type of publicity for which Harley Davidson might well have gladly handed Willie G Davidson over to the Mujahideen - and who could blame them? (No offence Willie).

Mr Turner spent six months a year in America: always Triumph's most important market. He had heard rumours about wild bunches of bikers who lived by their machines and rejected America's traditional values. The vast majority were ex-servicemen who were bored and possibly even unhinged which was the inevitable consequence of sending the wartime generation roaring over the skies of Germany day after day. They had shivered in skies three miles high and seen their friends plunge to their deaths whilst their own bombers droned on. Consequently it was never really their intention to return to a small town in the mid-west to sit on a production line watching Coca-Cola bottles pass by the million. Now they enjoyed the thundering motorcycle, the blast of the wind and the company of other 'devil may care' enthusiasts desperate to relieve their shared boredom. This was the freedom they had really fought for, something baseball and burgers just could not match.

Until then, celebrities like Rita Heyworth and MGM film star, Robert Taylor, had straddled Triumph motorcycles. Now Brando put Triumph on the map as the motorcycle of the 'bad boy'. Things would never be the same. The motorcycle subculture had attracted a worldwide audience and the dangerous became the highly undesirable as well. In 1953, Mr Turner was looking for respectable motorcycle enthusiasts. A motorcycle as a 'statement' or an advert for some deep sociologically justified 'chip on the shoulder' would have been treated with incomprehension or just simply ignored. But *The Wild One* was here to stay despite America's Triumph importer Bill Johnson of Johnson's Motors Ltd (Jo Mo) trying to stop the film and writing to the producer Stanley Kramer:-

> *It should be obvious that this film is calculated to do nothing but harm... the general impression will be left with those who see the film that a motorcyclist is drunken, irresponsible, just not nice to know...I urge you to give the foregoing comments your unbiased consideration, with a view to stopping production of this film.*

The Wild One made history for another reason. Up until then motorcycles had appeared on screen with their brand names obscured. For the first time in a major American film the motorcycle retained its tank badges. It was the brash but iconic Triumph logo with its long sweeping 'R' that was 'at the centre of this dark tale.' From here on the arrogant logo found its way onto the backs of black leather jackets of bad boys (and bad girls) the world over. It may as well have read 'trouble'.

There was doubtless much else on the minds of Britain's managers on such mornings in 1953, without having to contend with a mass of negative publicity. Only if you read *This England* magazine do you believe that 1950's England was a tranquil place in which the parish spinsters cycled through the early morning mist to do the church flowers and everyone knew their place. Indeed most felt their place should be elsewhere after the sacrifices of the war and to get there, they had to work. The awesome responsibility for providing that work fell on the shoulders of Mr Turner and others. He knew the importance of the dollar in keeping the workers in his 'little factory in England' fully employed. The pressure was on. Had counselling been invented it would have taken somebody rather brave to suggest to Mr Turner that he avail himself of its questionable benefits; a good blast on a Triumph invariably did the trick.

It is the eternal nature of motorcycles to enable their riders to 'get away from it' and 'break free from the crowd'. The word 'freedom' is prominent with generations of motorcyclists when asked why they risk life and limb by their non-motorcycling friends. From the dawn of motorised transport, the loud and unleashed motorcycle broke down the barriers and set the rider free. Restless souls the world over find tranquillity at speed and motorcycling metaphors are always about motion. From the time that the handlebars vibrate and the whole world unfolds, your worries are left behind to 'eat dirt'. However Mr Turner would have probably found it easier to identify with the words of Lawrence of Arabia when he wrote:-

> *The burble of my exhaust unwound like a cord behind me, soon my speed snapped it and I heard only the cry of the wind which my battering head split and fended aside.*

Mr Turner and his team at all levels in the factory would undoubtedly have felt the pressure to sell and the Gaffers' Gallop came at the right time. He and the outstanding American Dealer network were responsible for generating one million pounds worth of exports and Mr Turner had certainly earned his week on the road.

Whatever the short-term impact of *The Wild One*, things could have been worse. The film could have been made in Britain. Alas in 1953, this sceptred isle was on the cusp of a whole new genre of filmmaking. Out went the jolly japes of Ealing Comedies as *Saturday Night At The Movies* dealt with little rib ticklers whose collective sociological theme could be summed up as 'aint it crap bein' workin' class?' This genre culminated in the story of one of the lads from the legendary Ace Café who sold his Triumph and ran away to sea when he found his wife left crumbs in the bed! It was also probably why Mr Turner chose to stay away from the cinema on Sedwell Street, preferring to retire with a copy of *MotorCycling* magazine and his slippers instead. You can't blame him really: well, you watch *The Leather Boys* and you'll know what I mean.

BUZZARDS AND POP FESTIVALS

Next morning I rumbled onto the open road. The grey ceiling of cloud broke occasionally and the odd shaft of sunlight was an unconvincing reminder that this was supposed to be British Summer Time.

I had chosen to take my trip in June rather than October when Mr Turner originally went. This was on the basis that my ride would be more comfortable. Or so I thought.

I threw the Triumph around the bends that line the feet of the Mendips as buzzards hung in the breeze. I could have ridden all day on roads like these, and indeed in the days when this poem was penned would have been compelled to:-

> *Before the Roman came to Rye*
> *Or out to Severn strode,*
> *The rolling English drunkard*
> *Made the rolling English road.*

And I was grateful to him for that as a roll of images of hamlets and village greens were imprinted on my subconscious. There were too many to mention but all were the optimum size for the benefit of the human condition. There was time for people to pass the time of day and be part of a community. As I took a photograph of the village sign of Huish Episcopi, Paul, a fellow motorcyclist, came strolling down the road with his newspaper under his arm; he took one of my fundraising leaflets, which I thought no more of until a week later when 'Paul from Langport' came up on my 'Just Giving' website. He had kindly made a donation to 'a motorcyclist with matted hair and whiskers' who thought Huish Episcopi was a name dreamt up by mushroom heads from the Glastonbury Festival. And from here all roads lead to Glastonbury, or at least all mud-caked roads. As I came upon the outskirts of the town the sun shone on the Festival site and the stragglers. It all seemed very different twenty years ago when four of my fellow alumni drove a hired Mini Metro to get to the anarchic free festival at Stonehenge.

Then as now the town was full of traffic, and I was diverted around the site of a factory in the process of demolition. Glastonbury's shops specialise in tat for hippies and as I didn't need either a dream catcher or crystals, I gave the town centre a wide birth. I rode passed the farm where Tilly and I had stayed when we first got the Triumph. It was owned by an elderly army officer and his young wife who kindly gave us a room after enquiring, "Do you carry knives?" I had never been asked that before. As the old boy warmed up he fell into fits of hysteria when he had to give telephone directions to his next set of guests, a minibus full of clairvoyants. Quite made his day.

Outside of the town, I turned into the lane that ran out at the foot of Glastonbury Tor. Twenty years ago I'd rounded the foot of the Tor in that Metro when a crowd of Bikers on smooth powerful customised Japanese bikes swung out and passed with ease, their t-shirts flapping. You could not do that on the Enfield Bullet I then owned. I briefly wished that British bikes were as smooth and powerful. Happy days? These are better!

I parked my smooth and powerful Thunderbird at the foot of the Tor where we had once run up, alas not with a naked virgin on each arm. In a cottage further up the road an old man tended a beautifully kept garden bristling with canes and ranks of onions. I stood back and photographed the bike, as you do.

I never thought twenty years ago, as Triumph struggled on with a skeleton staff that by then was based in Devon, that all these years later I would be parking here on a 900cc superbike from a resurgent factory. In fact the only thought I had as we left Glastonbury all those years ago was what on earth we were going to tell the owner of the Metro when he found his aerial had been replaced with a coat hanger cum dream catcher.

THE OPEN ROAD

"Oh public road …you express me better than I express myself", or so said Walt Whitman, whoever he is. The sentiment is just as apt for anyone for whom a journey is underway as they get into the rhythm of life on the open road. By now Messrs Turner, Fearon and Masters were well into that rhythm on the third day.

Under blue skies and sunshine they headed north, making their way through the autumn air impressing the observers with the way in which they held together as a team. *MotorCycling* magazine recorded that there was:-

> *No straggling, no wandering, but a thoroughly convincing display of tidy riding with positions maintained as neatly through town traffic as on the open road.*

From Exeter they wended their way to Honiton having passed the tiny Exeter airport and the villages of Jack In The Green and Hand And Pen. Mixing metaphors Eric Headlam commented, 'These terriers have really got the bit between their teeth now'.

Whilst Mr Turner, perhaps mindful of their vulnerability to congestion gave the car-borne members something of a ribbing: "you tuck in behind and let us do the leading, you're so slow that you'll be wrecking our average".

The average speed of 36 mph over 163 miles sounds unimpressive today. But these were 1953's roads and the best of these in those happy pre-motorway days had been built by the Romans, not least as subsequent latter day governments always gave priority to the railways. And the Romans built their roads with longevity in mind and the Gaffers were among the many who subsequently made good time on them.

Austere times and an economy model or not, 'making good time' simply meant going fast. Speed and motorcycles always went together. Even Mr Turner recognised that rapidity featured high on his customer's list of priorities. In pursuance of a finely engineered motorcycle he produced models that were light, strong and fast, but he still refused to race them. However he was quite happy to watch other manufacturers pouring their money into racing teams at Oulton Park or on the Isle of Man. However, the businessman in him refused to spend Triumph's money on motor sport. Even so, as he led the way from Shepton Mallet to Melksham he would have been aware of how much progress was made on the racetrack, not least in the quality of tyres.

Mr Turner's route crossed the River Avon and the successes heaped upon his rivals by their use of a well-chosen tyre would remind him every inch of the way, as this is the home of Avon Tyres. Had he read *MotorCycling* magazine in the golden glow of an evening in the drawing room of the Imperial, as I like to think, he could have checked the adverts. A mere six pages in front of Triumph's own advert rang out the words:-

Avon - today's leading tyres

Mr Turner approached Melksham and the Avon factory that used the old mill on the river bank as its headquarters for over a century. The company supplied tyres to Norton racer Geoff Duke OBE. Number one in the world, every motorcyclist wanted to beat Geoff and their first step was to get a set of his tyres. Incredibly every motorcycle world champion between 1958 and 1963 chose Avon. In the publicity stakes only motorcycle manufacturers themselves benefited more.

Mr Turner would not budge even though the Americans wanted to race. As Triumph's former works manager, John Nelson recalls:-

ET was adamant that a racing bike would not go down the production line.

And during his leadership none did; at least not officially. Thus whilst some manufacturers wanted their machines to be seen as the fastest, Mr Turner wanted his to be reliable and economical as well. Indeed he insisted that they use the 'minimum amount of metal for the maximum amount of work'. It hardly sounds unique, but the success it produced both commercially and mechanically certainly was.

Passing the Holy Grail of motor racing tyres, Mr Turner left behind the Avon factory that would not even notice his passing, for they were too busy. Indeed that very year Mr Turner's old friend, the founder of Jaguar cars, Sir William Lyons, had his XK120s bring home the laurels from the Le Mans 24 hour sports car race on Avon tyres. Curiously Sir William saw his cars off from Jaguar's famous HQ at Browns Lane in Coventry and promptly headed north to spend the weekend on the Isle of Man, watching his first love, motorcycles at the TT races. Of course Triumph were not there. Then it seemed that lapping the island on a production motorcycle at the ungodly speed of one hundred miles per hour was beyond humanity's grasp. When it happened some years later, Avon got the laurels, curiously on a Triumph but by then Mr Turner had gone.

One might think Mr Turner stubborn in the face of such glittering publicity. However, in the fullness of time all his rivals were out of production, but Triumph remained.

In an age when men were men and kept their thoughts to themselves, it is not recorded if there was any self-doubt but perhaps it is unlikely. As he left the hallowed banks of the river Avon I suspect Mr Turner's main thoughts were about lunch.

The Gaffers pulled in to the Old Bell in Malmesbury where they witnessed a rural England in which the old order had not changed for a thousand years. The social and economic changes of town life were seen as superficial. Beyond the suburbs and onto the lanes, good solid old money governed as it always had done and always would do. Brogues and tweeds sold in sensible and steady quantities and would do so long after 'winkle pickers' had been forgotten. Thus when Mr Turner pulled up he became comfortably ensconced in the world of gently ticking grandfather clocks and striding Colonels who spoke in clipped tones.

The Old Bell was the HQ of the Badminton Hunt as well as a temple of the Masonic Order and had been in the same family for generations. They spawned local worthies and even hosted the Mayoral Banquet. All had served in the Royal Wilts Infantry; all had added a wing to the Old Bell and always flew the flag at half-mast when a monarch died. They really were like that in 'those days'. Still, in common with today a good long ride created a healthy appetite and once the Gaffers were seated the Terrier's engines

cooled as lunch was served. Another agreeable morning concluded with
Robert Fearon commenting:-

*I had almost forgotten what good fun motorcycling can be. Take the smells
for instance. You can see the countryside better from the saddle and smell it
too – which is more than you can do when you're driving a car. At one stage
this morning when we were passing through some cider apple country the smell
was worth bottling.*

At the Old Bell they may have been quaintly bonkers in brogues but
getting the pig to cross the road was no problem. Food miles were few, so
when you stopped in Wiltshire it was Wiltshire fayre you consumed

It is easy to think of time standing still with the golden autumn gathering
outside as they sat at their table blessed by the local harvest. Alas 'progress'
dictated that like Exeter, to the south and towns elsewhere, 'fast food'
was about to take over. However for the time being there were no plastic
wrapped soggy sandwich corners prepared three days previously: well, you
can imagine what Mr Turner would have had to say.

Refreshed the Gaffers stepped outside and pulled on their gauntlets as
Mr Turner ruminated:-

*You know, speaking purely as a rider, I think the little Terrier has got
something that is going to appeal to quite a lot of people.*

But perhaps not to people who used horse drawn vehicles which were still
commonplace, particularly in rural communities. The penetrating crack of
the single cylinder Terrier was enough to make any nervous old nag a little
frisky. And each day some such nag took the milk from nearby Cowage Farm
and braced itself for the 'hustle and bustle' of downtown Malmesbury in
order to drop its load off at the railway station. The dust had long settled and
the Gaffers had gone for good when the next delivery was made, sparing the
old nag so that the milk was delivered in this picture postcard way for some
time yet before being immortalised by ye olde tourist borde.

Straight back up the Fosse Way with its mile after mile of long unyielding
Roman road, running on little more than a whiff of petrol subjecting the
rider to a gentle but reassuring tremble through the handlebars. On roads
like this the bikes could cross continents but instead Bath, Cirencester and
the ever popular Stow-on-the-Wold had to suffice.

In the course of this journey the Gaffers would stop for the night a few
miles south of Mr Turner's home, a mock Tudor pile known as Abbotsvale.

There was ample space for the entire entourage to get lost amidst the corridors and high ceilinged rooms, but the Gaffers were destined for elsewhere.

Mr Turner's home life had not always been happy, something which he occasionally carried into the work place where more cautious, but less flamboyant assistants, propped up his occasional shortcomings as an engineer. However all this overlooks his sad early years, which may have created what it took to shape this most driven man.

On a dark night in 1939, Mr Turner's first wife was returning home with three friends. She and Mr Turner had much to look forward to. Now that success was his, Mr and Mrs Turner were planning a family, but Mrs Turner never made it home. The car in which she was travelling was involved in a collision and everyone in the car was killed. Mr Turner later recalled that on hearing of the news:-

> *I fainted away like a baby and coming to from that faint is one of the most painful recollections of my life, that will follow me to the grave.*

Mr Turner rattled around his mansion with no one but his driver Frank Griffiths for company. He threw himself at his work to escape the looming cloud of pain that only gradually lifted with the slow passage of time. Frank was there to serve at dinner parties, hold his shotguns and drive him at will. He was more than just a driver; he had seen his boss through his darkest hour. However it was probably Mr Turner's diabetes that was responsible for his famously short fuse and he would have completely failed at the people management courses of today. Indeed if Frank had ever had to appraise his boss they would probably have killed each other. Yet Frank stayed his loyal driver for decades, which probably says it all. Curiously moving as their relationship was, Frank still found himself irritated during their long lonely miles together when his boss would goad him to put his foot down. A spat would evolve into a full blown row in which Mr Turner would express the desire to demonstrate to Frank just how fast a particular route could be taken. Frank would then find himself relegated to the back seat as the wheels spun and Mr Turner fought with the steering wheel and gear stick to prove his point. Frank, who was no slouch as a driver would find to his disgust that Mr Turner had invariably shaved time off his journey. Alas Frank was at a disadvantage for if a magnificent Daimler V8 powered the vehicle in which they were travelling, his boss had designed it.

Frank's role in the Gaffers' Gallop has to be recorded because occasionally Mr Turner would rearrange the drivers and stick Frank on a Terrier to complete a hard days riding so that he could sleep off lunch in the walnut and leather cocoon of the Sunbeam. This allowed Frank to draw alongside the rear passenger window where his boss was contentedly snoring and tell him what he really thought about the terms of his employment.

Soon they rumbled into Stratford-upon-Avon. With the bikes warm and performing perfectly they were slowed by the rush hour traffic and a populace drawn to Birmingham like moths to a bright light. With more waterways than Venice and domino rows of suburban duplexes thrown up to receive the never ending migration of people from under the noses of the squire of Malmesbury and elsewhere. All a long way from the ticking grandfather clock in the Old Bell Inn and its gentle complaint of 'the price of staff these days'. Here one is dizzied 'with the hammering of presses, the clatter of engines and the whirling of wheels'.

This is the beating heart of the nation: the closer you got to it, the louder you felt that beat. It fed economic growth, threw up larger homes for the newly rich and eclipsed the landed gentry close to its pulse that did not dance to its rhythm.

Perhaps Frank Griffith had given up the Terrier to enable Mr Turner to ride triumphantly into the magnificent splendour of Leamington Spa. Villages witnessed their passing until they reached Warwick where their exhaust notes bounced off the medieval walls of Warwick Castle in the dying days of private ownership, before it passed forever into public hands.

Finally they pulled up outside the elegant Georgian pile on The Parade that is the Regent Hotel. The Gaffers all passed under the coat of arms supported by the Roman columns and were welcomed by yet another doorman. If you wanted staff now, then you had to be in industry; it pays better than even feudalism.

The night drew in, the gas-light world gently flickered and Pinewood Studios left a curious legacy: the notion that as the camera dimmed, the sound track crackled and the fires burned low, England was eternally content. We all knew our place, the wireless was switched off and we went to bed. With our own spouses. And then we were all fast asleep before the church bell chimed midnight. And nobody had sex.

AVON CALLING

Having already fallen behind Mr Turner I followed the road sign that pointed to Bradford-on-Avon. Underneath a graffiti artist had optimistically scribbled 'the place where dreams come true'.

I was looking for a rubber tyre factory which curiously did not feature on the tourist map. So I wound my way down the lanes until I finally found Melksham where the one-way system lead me comfortably to the vast complex that is the home of my sponsor, Avon Tyres. I duly swung in through the factory gates and pulled up right outside their ivy clad head office. I was late. I crept into the plush foyer where I was met, not surprisingly with the whiff of rubber. Subtle spotlights fell on framed pictures of modern cars and motorcycles still picking up the laurels. In a glass cabinet was a model of a Formula One racing car and an array of trophies. I was all alone for a long time in what is the centre of the universe, if you are into rubber.

The factory as an entity is slowly fading from view in Britain. Indeed it has not been loved for over a century, whilst the homes of mine owners, slave traders and Highland lairds are visited by the great grandchildren of their exploited victims. Their collective thoughts focus on the seat at the head of the table in the great hall oblivious to the peasant stock depicted in the sentimental paintings hanging from the walls. The happy rustic kitchen, children with rosy cheeks, the dead ducks on the table fit for a still life and not a sign of rickets anywhere. That vast numbers are no longer living exhibits for his Lordship's pleasure is thanks to the industrial revolution and the factory. Curiously there are no sour old dames with twin sets, stood imperiously behind rope cordons to prevent tourists touching the workbenches in factories or lifting the smutty calendars off the workshop walls. Alas factories have played a far more significant role in Britain's greatness than big pads in the country surrounded by pheasants, but they just aren't pretty.

It was lunchtime and there was a mass exodus of the overalled through the factory gates. I strode over to the intercom and explained the purpose of my visit. There was a deathly silence until the security lock clicked and the head of marketing, Sarah McRoberts welcomed me to the factory and in her lunch hour too. Thank you Sarah, or should that be sorry Sarah.

With so many celebs doing things on bikes and attracting vast publicity for their sponsors, I could well understand if Sarah felt that a solicitor from suburbia on a week's holiday was the baddest of bum deals she had ever been persuaded to back. Still she was not going to ask for her tyres back now and I got a cup of tea.

I was about to commence the factory tour courtesy of Avon employee Neil Crooke: a fellow motorcyclist and recent father around my own age. The tour started at the top of the factory from where you could see the vast complex. "Quite a long way up those stairs isn't it," said Neil, turning around to see me panting on my hands and knees. When I finally staggered to my feet, I surveyed the scene. It was entirely organic in the true sense of the word. There was the sandstone watermill that stood on the banks of the Avon since the year dot and witnessed the arrival of barges of cotton and Indian rubber. From where we stood every single style of factory was splayed out before us, exemplifying each period of steady success in the company's long history. The Victorian red brick gradually gave way to progress as the factories evolved into the prefabricated at the perimeter of the site. The occasional chimney reached for the sky, vents whirred and forklift trucks drove from warehouse to wagon and back. Up here on the factory roof close to the clouds, the sound of activity was remote and easily swept off in the breeze. People moved like ants just to put tyres on the motorcycles of the world.

I had always thought that making tyres was simple. You got a solution of hot rubber, poured it into a mould and waited for it to cool down. Lawdy, how they will laugh in Melksham when they read this.

From the heights of the factory we followed the route of raw rubber via vast tubes and pipes on the top floor of the building that acted like a giant chemistry set. On the lower floors its temperature was carefully controlled through machines that exhibited constant dials. A boffin in overalls watched the process with his back to us. Neil leant over and whispered, "he's the fourth generation of his family to do this job". And he made my tyres too.

From there we swept through buildings with sacks of additives being measured and added to what would become the tyres that move the discerning. In my mind the whole process slowly merged together with rubber being rolled out in great lengths as it took on an improved form. At each stage Neil handed me a rubber off-cut and I felt the evolution of the crude to the refined.

Another factory block and Neil passed me another strip of rubber that by now was literally sticky. That is what you want underneath you when you are whipping around the Isle of Man at insane speeds and angles.

From a distance I watched one of the workers at a machine. He was completely unaware that Neil and I had entered the vast complex. With a degree of skill and care that would be the envy of surgeon and tailor alike he placed strips of rubber at crisis-crosses along the length of tread.

"Why is he doing that?"

"So that whichever direction you travel you've always got grip."

"But I only travel forwards."

"Yes, but if you ever lose control you want it back as soon as possible."

Three centuries ago the criss-cross man could have been the subject of high art. Instead of having a motorcyclist who looked like a tramp behind him it could have been William Coleridge with an easel. Throughout the industrial revolution, scientific and manufacturing endeavour was seen as part of an extension of the natural world. To harness the natural forces of fire and water and bring them together brought one closer to nature itself. In that eighteenth century painting that went by the catchy title of *An Iron Forge Viewed From Without*, Joseph Wright depicts the glowing faces of a family by the fire of a forge in a derelict mill nestling in the Derwent Valley. But the passage of time has been unkind to industry and it became the new bogeyman. By the forties, Stanley Spencer was producing paintings of welders on the Clyde cooped up like battery hens. The romance gave way to 'realism' (miserable stuff) that cast industry in the role of the new exploiter.

We left the criss-cross man and passed through the ranks of pristine tyres as the air hung thick with rubber. Tyres were being blown up, tested and rotated as machines thrust them back and forth and no one noticed our passing. In the distance I spotted what looked like a couple of musical symbols mounted on a machine and as we approached I asked Neil, "What are those?"

"The mould for Avon Speedmasters, they've been there since the forties".

This was the very same mould that made the tyres for my father's Vincent and all Geoff Duke's TT victories. The logo was distinct from all other logos in the factory being art deco in style. The same logo appeared in old motorcycle magazines, on the billboards at Le Mans and even on my old Scalectrix. And you can still buy these very tyres today; well I was impressed.

Sadly the time for me to go had arrived and I was photographed outside the head office. Neil would return to his home and family and I would wait a week to see mine. However we had both concluded that with careful management we might be able to persuade our wives to allow us to put our respective children in a sidecar for the family holiday. I have since wondered if Neil's plans got any further than mine.

Out of town and heading north I snapped back the throttle, gave the back end a little wiggle and went round a bend like the bike was on rails.

Back on the Fosse Way, the wild and woolly South West gently eased its grip on the landscape to give way to middle England. Perhaps when the Gaffers passed this way it was less picture post card twee and by Stow-on-the-Wold the wellingtons and Land Rovers were all too clean for my liking. I was on my own and unlike Mr Turner, without the motorcycle press in tow. The wind blew and the rush hour was finally in full swing and I carried on relentlessly north. I finally reached Stratford-upon-Avon and went in search of a place to rest my weary head. I was unaware that Stratford's entry in *The Rough Guide To England* reads:-

Stratford-upon-Avon is an unremarkable town with a pedigree that is unexceptional... (and as a consequence of being Shakespeare's birthplace) this ordinary little place is nowadays all but smothered by package tourist hype and tea-shoppe quaintness, representing the worst of England - Land Heritage marketing.

I slowly rode down a leafy road in search of a campsite noting the innumerable caravan sites protected by 'No Campers' signs. How I hankered after the grunginess of Cornwall and the magnificence of the Logan Rock.

I found myself in a part of Stratford that owed more to Dickens than Shakespeare. The locals were:-

Bran new people with a bran new house in a bran new quarter ....everything about (them) was spick and span new...

A little man wearing a Pringle sweater mowed his lawn with studied intensity. His neighbour vacuumed out his car. Another shampooed his cast concrete statue.

Back in town it was Repsville. The car parks in front of the guesthouses were crammed full with budget BMWs. Some proudly sported their three star accommodation status signifying a TV on a piece of angle iron and a poky en-suite shower in a cupboard. Could I? No. I returned down the 'bran new' quarter where Captain Pringle was emptying his grass box...with gloves on!

At the end of the road was the magnificent Stratford Youth Hostel. I used to be sniffy about people who used hostels when they reached them by petrol power. However, by the time I passed through its front doors I was desperate. At the reception, I enquired if I could put my tent up in the grounds, as the YHA used to adopt this laisez faire approach to accommodating all travellers that was part of the movements appeal. The young lady looked at me, backed off; her nostrils splayed and exhaled air. I wondered what was wrong with her. She backed off again and I braced myself for either flames or a bovine charge. Alas Veronika just said, "aah noo" a couple of times and passed me a leaflet titled 'Camping In Wales'. I guess that summed up Stratford and so I headed out of town, over the swollen river.

I was back on the road and in a middle England of garden centres and plastic flowerpots where the demand for campsites seems lower than anywhere else in the country. And then when I escaped the beaten track it all changed. The lanes wended their way lined with dogwort, punctuated by patches of grit washed onto the road. Silver streams of rainwater ran in the gutter as the cloud occasionally parted and let them carry off the sun's reflection. Beyond the shaggy hedgerows lay rolling farmland; paradise not entirely lost.

I turned onto a bridge over a stream, through an avenue of trees and pulled up by a red telephone box in the middle of a caravan site. A friendly one with old caravans, chickens, children and a toilet block with leaded windows. The genial owner invited me to put my tent up in front of the stately pile with the words "don't worry mate, the river never floods". And so I settled under a weeping willow, ate a stale pie out of my pannier (or at least that is what I thought it was) and turned my thoughts to the morrow. I would visit a place whose acres spawned a legend. A place where a noble and very British battle was fought out between a worker's co-operative and the economic might of a Japanese industry against the backdrop of an ambivalent British government. A place where the surrounding lanes resonated to the sound of an incongruously well dressed Mr Turner riding flat out on one of his latest creations. The place that for forty one years was the home of the Triumph motorcycle at the geographical dead centre of England. Tomorrow I was going to Meriden.

THE CENTRE OF THE UNIVERSE

Bob Fearon had not noticed Mr Turner step along side him and study him intently. He was fastening down the pockets of his Barbour jacket prior to stepping out of the Regent Hotel when he caught a glimpse of Mr Turner out of the corner of his eye.

"ET", came his familiar acknowledgement. It was never Edward.

Mr Turner did not speak but redirected his gaze to where Bob had previously been staring so intently; the statue of Queen Victoria surrounded by parked motorcycles.

"You can't really be concerned about that lot Fearon."

"Not at all E T."

Mr Turner was in a curious mood. Bob was aware that looking at another manufacturer's motorcycles could be akin to adultery.

"I'm glad to hear it Fearon. They're all lawn mowers. Loud, without elegance and clearly made for those who've little pride in how they arrive. I don't know why they keep making them. The Americans won't buy them."

Mr Turner spoke thoughtfully and quietly as he noted the makes: James, Greeves and the odd BSA Bantam.

"Have you ever been to America, Fearon?"

He only had time to open his mouth before Mr Turner interjected.

"Time you did. That's the future, where people have to make things that are more than just nuts and bolts. You've got to have flair to stand out from the crowd if you're going to survive these days. Mark my words Fearon, there will only be one make of motorcycle around that statue fifty years from now and it will be mine."

Bob Fearon did not feel rebuked but he was struck by the conviction with which Mr Turner delivered his message.

He glanced back at the statue. A young man and his girlfriend were strolling by. As they did so he was pointing out the names on the petrol tanks. Quite why men think their wives or girlfriends are interested in such things is completely lost on womankind. In trying to picture the scene fifty years hence, Bob Fearon could only surmise that men would still hold that mistaken belief. And if Mr Turner was right, and he usually was, it would be a Triumph at the Queen-Empress' feet.

Immaculately booted and Barboured they were the very embodiment of the gentleman motorcyclist. Soon they were all counted out as Mr Turner ruminated on the prospect of prejudicing their one hundred miles per gallon target by their fast average speed.

"No pressing on today – we're aiming at an average of not more than thirty two miles in the hour".

With that the engines were started as the wind stood fair for Carlisle and the Gaffers moved out. En route Mr Turner would ride close to Meriden, the location of the Triumph factory where he would spend twenty-two years of his working life and which would become imbued with his firm fingerprint in every corner, as if it were his own personal fiefdom.

Triumph had been bombed out of their first factory in Coventry by the Luftwaffe. Mr Turner had initially resisted moving to Meriden and this was the first of a series of major decisions over which he was difficult, but the others were far more significant.

The second was his aversion to increasing the size of his 1936 500cc Speed Twin. It was a brilliant motorcycle and in his view a twin cylinder engine should not exceed 500cc. The Americans pressured him for a 650cc and in 1949 he relented and built the first Thunderbird 650. Four years before the Gaffers' Gallop he pulled off another publicity coup, this time in France. Before leaving Meriden, 'ace salesman' Neale Shilton and fellow riders stopped for a photograph at the factory gates on four very elegant and entirely modern machines that looked like speed even when stood still. They had pulled back and slightly turned down handlebars that looked like the horns of a raging bull. However the other development owed much to art deco and 1940's science fiction. The nacelle at the top of the forks out of which those handlebars grew was a casque borrowed from aircraft design. It tidied up all those loose cables and held the headlamp. But in Mr Turner's hands it was a thing of beauty, as if shaped by nature and lined with chrome that added to the overall impression of god like speed. Like all of Mr Turner's motorcycles his finishing touches were a matter of art.

The next time Mr Turner saw his Thunderbirds they were flying around the banked track at Montlhery. On the final lap all three exceeded a constant one hundred miles per hour. This was available from a production motorcycle that any working man could purchase with prudence in 1949!

That record breaking ride made the BBC evening news and on their return the riders rode through the cheering streets of Coventry. Meanwhile back at the factory they were packing the new record breaking Thunderbirds by the ship load, most bound for America.

At around this time a call was put through from a Hollywood studio to the warehouse of Triumph dealers, Johnson's Motors (Jo Mo) in Pasadena, California. Amidst the crates from England was a sales manager called Don Brown. He took the call that turned out to be from the agent of an unknown actor called Terence 'Steve' McQueen who wanted a Triumph. Like the rest of Jo Mo he was suspicious of 'Hollywood types'. Don recalled to the author for the first time publicly in over half a century:-

> I kept saying no, but in the end I got Steve to purchase the bike at cost. In fact he was in the TV program called 'Wanted Dead Or Alive', a sort of Western. He purchased a new Triumph from me and I delivered it to him at Universal Studios in the city. That was Steve's first new bike.

Long before Jo Mo linked the Triumph brand to the man who became known as the 'King Of Cool', business was brisk. Court battles to allow imports were won, profits soared and Mr Turner looked after the all important American market. Consequently he was doing rather well whilst the rest of Britain was better acquainted with the need for austerity; but Mr Turner never kept himself so remote from his market that he did not realise this. And consequently the 150cc Terrier, star of the Gaffers' Gallop was born.

Whilst Britain wanted 100 mpg out of the single cylinder Terrier, America wanted 200 mph out of the twin cylinder bikes, and so throughout the fifties Mr Turner's finely balanced engine was successfully tuned for ever increasing speeds. Triumphs were also seen as raffish and fast in America, which protected them from the sales slump that subsequently affected the rest of the industry. Inadvertently or otherwise, the Triumph brand had taken its first steps towards becoming linked to popular culture, largely because this 'little factory in England', so far away from America's heart-beat, kept its finger on Uncle Sam's pulse.

Back at Meriden the factory was a special place because of the peculiar magic that unifies a body of people behind a common cause and what left their production line was made for them and their kind: regular guys. However it wasn't all good and over time the union barons managed to carve out their own little empires; incredibly Mr Turner never even met a shop steward in their official capacity. Consequently the film *I'm Alright Jack* remained a comedy, even if Mr Turner had never had time to sit down and watch it.

The Gaffers had not yet recognised this turn of events in 1953 when popular culture still meant Bingo Halls and Blackpool and Mr Turner's staff still did as they were told. Thus under the brilliant blue skies of autumn they rode their motorcycles, designed by Mr Turner, made by his workforce in a factory run entirely by him. Little did they know that in less than ten years the job of management would be recognised as a separate and remote 'profession'. The notion that people who knew nothing about motorcycles, and even boasted that they neither liked them nor their riders, should be suitable to run an industry would never have been entertained by an entirely sane mind. And the early fifties were an entirely sane and sober era with Triumph still a small independent company. However by the mid fifties Triumph had been sold to the giant BSA motorcycle group with no immediate alteration in Triumph's or Mr Turner's autonomy. He bagged a quarter of a million pounds in the deal. Private schools in Switzerland for his daughters and a house in the Bahamas became part of his lifestyle.

Along with the sale proceeds of Triumph, the company's owner, Jack Sangster secured a seat on the BSA parent company board. In a mesmeric twist in fortunes, the man who had sold a cottage industry to a corporate giant was about to wield the dagger and wear the crown. Jack was a motorcycling tycoon who had overheard some disparaging remarks about his penchant for the open road whilst sat behind a large leather chair at his London club.

Apparently a motorcyclist was not the 'right sort' to be on the board of directors. From that moment on he set out to take over the group and did so with calculating ruthlessness even if it ultimately evolved into a performance fit for an Ealing comedy. To understand how comical, one has to appreciate the times in which we lived. As a nation we had nought but the occasional banana boat to provide our luxuries. The government's responsibility to teach us how to be thrifty fell upon the Ministry of Information. A number of public service films were released in which a gilt edged English accent consoles the nation's ladies and urges them not to bemoan the state of their wardrobes with the words:-

Ladies, we don't need Paris fashion houses. Why, every man with a knife and an off-cut of carpet can make the lady in his life a hat fit for Ascot.

And there she appeared modelling a hat fashioned by blokes with old lino and a Stanley knife rather than Yves Saint Lauren.

Those blokes did not get off lightly either as they were turned out to their vegetable patches to tend their turnips, desperate not to mention the shortage of fertilizer:-

Gentlemen, we all know what happens twenty minutes after a pint of pale ale. Save it for the garden.

Vigorous root crops followed, as well dressed ladies promenaded the bomb damaged streets attired in old carpet. With all this poverty around, one Lady Norah Docker honestly believed she could lift the nation's spirits by showing the masses how comfortable life could be if only they were as rich as she was, a demonstration she tried to charge to the BSA motorcycle group, whose chairman was conveniently her hubby, Sir Bernard Docker. Norah's argument was that she brought publicity to the group, which included Triumph and the Royal Family's favourite conveyance, Daimler cars. Norah ordered two of these and had them gold plated. Then at a price equivalent to the cost of twenty worker's terraces she had them upholstered in Zebra skin. Norah was bonkers, but in her mind absolutely right. If you gold plate your car you are bound to attract attention to yourself in the same way that you will if you bath in chocolate. The truth was that Norah was never out of the papers, flaunting her wonga for what she thought was everyone's enjoyment.

We bring glamour and happiness into drab lives. The working class loves everything I do.

And Norah got close to that working class when she invited a bus-load of miners onto Sir Bernard's 878 ton yacht, *Shemara*. As their stomach's rumbled, they sat there breathing life into their soggy Woodbines whilst witnessing Norah dancing the hornpipe for their benefit.

Back at the BSA boardroom, Jack Sangster had discovered that whilst she was shaking her butt in the faces of hungry miners she was going through the firm's money. She was on the cusp of opening a gold showroom in Paris to which she would drive in one of her Daimlers, whilst wearing a gold dress, mink cape and mink rimmed hat. As this would inevitably put the Dockers on the front pages, then by association BSA motorcycles would also benefit and they should foot the bill. Or not, as Jack Sangster thought and promptly moved to finish the Dockers. Not only did he remove Sir Bernard as Chairman but booted him off the board completely. The following day the world descended on the Docker's comical press conference at which they poured out their hearts whilst quaffing pink champagne. Tears in eyes, cigar in hand, Sir Bernard huffed and puffed, "I've been sacked, sacked, sacked", which rather indicates that he had finally got the message, but Norah had to wade in:-

> *It's not the loss of the gold cars that makes me feel like this. And weren't they fun? They were my children. No it's the lovely Party I was planning for 25,000 BSA workers for my fiftieth birthday on June 23rd. A tip top affair – and now that's off.*

Norah saved the best till last,

> *How could they do this to him after seventeen years? Why, he is such a hard worker that he had a through line to the firm from our yacht.*

The TV cameras rolled, microphones bristled and the headlines were prepared. Sadly Daimlers were no longer discreet motors of good taste and Norah's wheels had upstaged the House of Windsor at the Old Nags of Ascot once too often. Her eccentric publicity scheme had backfired and out of the exit of Buck House drove the last Royal Daimler and through the entrance a new Rolls Royce, whence the marque has remained ever since.

The press were enthralled as were the public behind a cordon outside the conference. The more the Dockers babbled away, the dafter they seemed. Norah had had enough and tripped down the steps and out onto the street where she exchanged incomprehensible glances with a public sporting Axminster headwear and nursing the largest turnips in Europe. She was off with the words, "Actually, I've always preferred Bentleys".

Jack had sold Triumph to BSA as the first step to retiring; becoming Chairman was only necessary to dampen Norah's Hornpipe. In 1961 he duly stepped down as Chairman himself and from now on a new breed of manager, invariably a 'consultant', would run the industry. As if by way of an omen the year of record profits under Sangster was immediately followed by a significant slump the following year.

The world was changing and Mr Turner might have doubted if it was for the better. Years previously he had been on the Gaffer's Gallop to see if the company's smallest model was good enough to carry Triumph's proud name. He would share the same road as his customers; experience the same performance, discomfort and sense of freedom. If the bike failed to perform he would be the first to know. He believed in symmetry, an optimum size and a minimum of 20,000 trouble free miles from a new model. Consequently Triumphs were handsome, smooth and so reliable that many police forces took them 'around the clock'. This was a product of the 'just get on with it' school of leadership and those born out of a new fashionable school would have a hard act to follow.

The first introduction to this new breed of leader from the fashionable school came about in circumstances of mystery and behind Mr Turner's back. While he was away, Triumph's sales director, Neale Shilton, had received instruction from Jack Sangster that he and senior executives meet at Mallory Park racing circuit and assemble all the models from across the range. Neale was waiting at the circuit entrance when the nose of one of Jack's Bentley Continentals emerged through the mist. The unassuming chairman whose charm was legendary, duly apologised for keeping Neale waiting and his unknown passenger bade him lead on. In moments Jack had his riding kit on and was enjoying himself on the Mallory circuit on board a 650 Triumph. Later in the club house the mystery guest spotted Neale's regimental tie and his first words to him were "have you served in my regiment?" Subsequently Jack introduced the new Vice Chairman to the assembled group of seasoned and successful industry men. He was an ex-Brigadier and accountant by the name of Eric Turner; no relation to Edward Turner by either blood or inclination. The Brigadier sported a Colonel Blimp moustache and had a vigorous crop of oily dyed hair. His manner of addressing his 'troops' owed more to the hapless Colonel than a man familiar with the importance of first impressions. He responded to Jack's invitation to comment on the range of assembled motorcycles by promptly advising that he did not like motorcycles and did not like those gathered about them. Remarkably, one is still in production today.

It was an odd way to start what would hopefully be a fruitful relationship. Perhaps it came about as the urgency of the 'export or die' era subsided. This occurred because of the efforts from an earlier decade when, at least at Meriden, people liked what they made. Perhaps also, some of the assembled guests could remember that autumn morning in October 1953 when the Gaffers moved through the traffic of Leamington Spa with near military precision. The weather was unseasonably mild as they made their short way towards Coventry. To the north-west was both the largest car and motorcycle industry on earth. They all knew each other; some had served together during the war and made a history for which they felt mankind would be forever grateful. Whenever they dined together they still draped the walls with the Union Jack and had a top table that was slavishly devoted to a social order.

And the Terriers rumbled on with Mr Turner content but never complacent.

The subsequent decline of Britain has exercised academics in seeking a common denominator behind the nation's post war performance, and the Trades Unions invariably fit the bill. Indeed Mr Turner would avoid Birmingham wherein hours earlier the sun had risen over a town riddled with closed shops, restrictive practices and occasional communist inclinations. But there are a multitude of reasons for Britain's perplexing post war performance and the selection of its leaders played its part. The distinguished historian Corelli Barnet considered what was the 'right sort of chap' to be an industrial leader in fifty's Britain and noted:-

> At the summit of the industrial system stood an elite predominately blessed with the accent of the officers' mess: men bowler hatted or Homburged, wearing suits of military cut either bespoke or at least bought from such approved outfitters as Aquascutum or Simpsons of Piccadilly: gentlemen indeed, confident of manner, instantly recognisable by stance or gesture.

Mr Turner was however an exception to the rule, although he put on a good show at concealing it. He would not have bothered with social bearing in America where a new empire was emerging based, in theory, on merit.

However the need to fit this particular bill resulted in 58% of directors being from public school, with Eton, Harrow and Winchester alone accounting for 8%. So concerned were they in some quarters that they actually carried out research on the subject.

In the 1850s, Britain engaged the 'world's best practice' in commerce and manufacturing. A century later the notion that 'you can't teach management' was being questioned. Various studies concluded that managers generally were '…little better than ill-trained amateurs self-taught on the job'. Corelli placed great emphasis on education and management studies. For those working in the millennium where the preponderance of graduates in everything has totally spent the intellectual currency of a degree, in a work environment of people with jobs of unidentifiable use or purpose, there has to be a third way. Perhaps that third way was making its own way around the outskirts of Birmingham in the autumn of 1953 on board a Triumph Terrier.

Mr Turner's thoughts drifted to the Meriden factory, the location of which had caused so much ill feeling between himself and Jack Sangster. When Coventry had been blitzed, Triumph went up in flames and needed a new factory. Some have suggested that the emollient Sangster kept Mr Turner on for just long enough for him to oversee the move. Sangster (Hurstpierpoint College) then summarily dismissed Mr Turner (Ongar Grammar), which may simplify the nature of their troubled relationship down class lines. However when Mr Turner's children arrived he had each of them privately educated which may reflect his thinking better than anything else. And into the millennium the descendants of Mr Turner wondered if his failure to approach the City for funding for his numerous inventions was down to a lack of contacts or social confidence, both of which Jack Sangster possessed in abundance. Either way, Jack Sangster and Mr Turner were soon reunited, only to fall out over a company known as ET Developments Limited that owned the intellectual property rights to Mr Turner's numerous inventions that Jack Sangster wanted. Perhaps such difficulties arise no matter how you select your leaders.

If the Brigadier had any intellectual property worth retaining it has been lost to history. He was, in fairness a 'leader', destined to see the bigger picture and preside over the direction of the whole industry. However some years after the Gaffers' Gallop it was Mr Edward Turner who went to Japan and accurately predicted that the Japanese were about to become a fierce rival, to which the Brigadier seemed unconcerned. By then the BSA group, consisting also of Triumph and Ariel motorcycles, was one of the nation's biggest concerns with seventy-nine subsidiaries. Sadly the art of 'getting a move on' was lost. The engineers who had run this empire up to that level of success were being put aside. Gone were the days when the management team looked upon accountants as 'some sort of clerks'. Those were the days of the Gaffers' Gallop when Mr Turner had managed to fill the order books and the future looked certain and prosperous. Subsequently teams of consultants moved into this profitable but archaic structure and sought to make it look more orderly, on paper at least. Those who had been groomed within the industry over a lifetime were now expected to step aside whilst teaching some starry eyed graduate how to take their own job off them. One Chief Designer and former Director of Norton Motorcycles, Bert Hopwood, listened as a highly paid consultant extolled the notion that managers should know as little about the product as possible. Bert queried how the accountants had come to inherit the biggest motorcycle industry on earth if that was right, and he was not a man to ignore. Bert was a thorough engineer in compliment to Mr Turner's flamboyance. While Mr Turner presided over Triumph's move to a 650cc twin, Bert presided over BSA's move in the same direction. He was also the most appropriate successor to Mr Turner's crown but his thinking wasn't fashionable as he noted the disbelief of the rising Japanese industry that the Brits were:-

...busy embarking on the madness of management consultancy rather than getting on with the job of work.

Sentiment is all very well but the motorcycle industry was an untidy and traditional old club. Even if there is ample research to show that people with untidy desks are more productive than those with tidy ones, change was due. If you are desk bound, Victorian red brick factories look untidy. Indeed, many of these companies did not even have a management chart and the consultants would have been shocked to find the Norton managing director, Gilbert Smith, personally carving the daily meat joint in a factory dining room manned by staff who knew their racing heroes but had never met a time and motion whiz kid.

The years passed and the political sound bite that defined the coming era was Harold Wilson's proclamation that we lived in 'The Britain that is going to be forged in the white heat of this (technological) revolution'. All that sounded right in an age that was still about bus trips to the coast, tired holiday camps and a public obsessed with the new. Harold created a Ministry for Technology and appointed Anthony Wedgwood Benn as its head whereon he acquired the nickname, 'Wedgie The Whiz'. Wedgie's job was arguably the most significant post in government giving him a portfolio over outer space, although he ended up redesigning postage stamps and insulting the Queen when he sought to remove her head. However the pop group, The Tornados had a much broader perspective when they shared the nation's fascination for the Telstar satellite and promptly named an instrumental after it. All this went on above the heads of the Chelsea Pensioners who could still be seen lining the park benches in the capital. They could explain why they fought in the Boer War but not why The Beatles had been awarded the MBE. Before plunging once more into sentiment about the fifties, it is worth remembering that during the week of the Gaffer's Gallop, there were two versions of the same song at the top of the 'hit parade'; *How Much Is That Doggie In The Window*? Some change cannot come soon enough.

Like every post industrial nation, Britain's economy had to change, that much everybody agreed on, including Mr Turner who by the mid-sixties was on the cusp of retirement. However, having a fashionable opinion, but being clueless as to why, is an inadequacy borrowed from the world of modern art. To straight talking Midlanders such opinions stimulated one word by way of response and although accurate, it is not very polite.

Into this sea of ferment steamed Triumph's new dynamic salesman called Harry Sturgeon. Riding roughshod over Mr Turner's policy of keeping demand up by limiting supply (the life long policy of Ferrari) he increased output by 40 percent over three years. But Harry was no production engineer and engine units piled up in every corner of the factory and ultimately in a marquee on the grass lawn whilst awaiting trucks to take them to the docks. This put strain on everyone including one member of the Meriden staff who actually died mid-telephone conversation with a supplier. When cautioned against his policy Sturgeon advised Bert Hopwood that he was a '…professional manager and must take decisions without wasting time listening to the arguments of other people'. While all this was happening Honda motorcycles, having listened, were poised to conquer the world.

Amidst all this chaos Mr Turner left and for many, despite glories yet to come, 1964 signalled the beginning of the end. No longer would new appointees receive a personal letter from Mr Turner himself with the instruction to 'conduct yourself in a manner which will lend prestige to yourself and the company'. Neither would their opinions be courted with the words 'I have brought you here to discuss colour finishes for next year's models and these are the ones I have decided'. Mr Turner would stay on in a consultancy capacity and on the main board along with Jack Sangster, but Triumph looked very vulnerable alongside the mighty BSA and a management that wanted to make things 'neat and tidy' on paper.

Mr Turner's farewell dinner was at the George Hotel in Solihull and was presided over by Neale Shilton who had an understandably uneasy feeling about Triumph without Mr Turner. At the conclusion of his career Sir Winston Churchill commented on the Britons whom he led thus:-

*A body of people with the heart of a lion. I had the good fortune to be called
on to give them the roar.*

Much the same can be said of Mr Turner and his 'little factory in England'.

The sixties were by now in full swing and as a consequence of under
investment, British motorcycles had an easy to mend, self-reliant charm
about them. More by fault than design, they became emblematic of
masculinity which combined with the impact of *The Wild One*, guaranteed
that they were the first choice for the hooligan. England's coastal resorts
bore the brunt of their mobility as one after the other exploded with bank
holiday riots causing World War Two veterans to question in the letters
columns if their sacrifice had all been worth it. British motorcycles were
now beyond the pale and, never one to miss an opportunity, the motorcycle
press filled with adverts from one oriental rival that read, 'you meet nicer
people on a Honda'. The die was cast.

The Brigadier continued to march his consultants through Mr Turner's
empire and promptly sought to remove the human face of the Meriden
factory. No holidaying families would ever drop in to find eager young
apprentices to help get them back on the road. It was closed to the public.
If the workforce had any doubts about the merits of the new style of
management, they could rest assured that the Brigadier and his team were
financiers of 'international renown'. Thus when a pay dispute was being
settled, Harry Sturgeon burst into the meeting eager to ensure that his
production targets were not prejudiced. Showing the old boys a thing or two
about modern management he rolled up his sleeves and started the bidding
at more than the unions were actually seeking! Quite what these financiers
were renowned for was becoming clear and a new nickname was emerging
locally for Triumph; The Mint.

Harry's successor, Lionel 'Jolly' Jofeh, was a fatal accompaniment to
the Brigadier and together they would build on that renown. Meanwhile
the former hero of the Gaffers' Gallop, Bob Fearon resigned as the trickle
turned into a stream of resignations coinciding with the arrival of newcomers
strolling around under the Brigadier and Jolly. The 'yes men' had arrived
and for those remaining Bert Hopwood noted:-

*It is unforgivable that these men, many of whom had left positive marks
in a successful industry should now find themselves with bosses who knew
nothing about motorcycles, but worse than this almost without exception, were*

regarding their new found way of life as some sort of academic mission into the
primitive back wood of two wheeled philosophy.

In the evolving post industrial age that 'academic mission' was justified by
the scourge of modern business: meetings. These took up rather a lot of time
and the BSA group soon had more meetings than motorbikes. Bert recalls:-

We were reorganised, coordinated, charted and paperised to such a degree that
our offices simply were not big enough.

In keeping with the spirit of the times, Triumph's advertising manager,
Ivor Davies, found these bright eyed graduates changing his title to export
market development manager, export development manager, market product
marketing manager, product planning advisor, deputy sales manager UK, PA
to the general manager of Triumph and then advertising manager once again.

There was an increasing feeling amongst the work force that Meriden
was being deliberately 'buggered up' so that there was an excuse to close the
factory down and bring the industry in line with a consultant's flip chart.
Indeed one designer noted of Jolly, 'he literally hated Triumph's success and
seemed quite determined to make Triumph the underdog'. At the Triumph
Christmas party they would entertain friendly motorcycle journalists until
Jolly promptly banned their attendance in favour of three BSA executives.
Jolly then commenced the happy gathering by merrily threatening to sack
anyone who favoured Triumph over BSA. Jolly's real problem was that
Triumph had just won the prestigious Queen's Award for Exports and the
Brigadier's Empire was only kept afloat by 'Meriden Monday' when the
profits made at Triumph were taken from them to subsidise the entire
industry. Irked by Triumph's success, Jolly rounded on Neale, "Shilton, if
you possessed any real business acumen, you would not be in this industry".
However Jolly was to find out that Neale had skills as an after-dinner speaker
when called upon to give the Christmas address. He suggested that Jolly take
a look at the book of 'profits' and rounded up his Christmas message:-

God rest ye Meriden Gentlemen let nothing you dismay,business is good at
Triumph but dreadful at BSA.

However it felt like Jolly had Neale 'by the balls' and whilst his sarcasm
was entirely understandable, Jolly was still his boss. It was no more
comfortable for the litigant in the famous 'caught' case of America. The
unfortunate naked motorcyclist was out on his Triumph when he was broad
sided by an uninsured drunk in a pick up. They do some funny things out of

town and he duly flew over the handlebars *sans* manhood and subsequently appeared in court in a nappy. Someone had to take the rap and as a foretaste for the future of litigation in which personal responsibility does not feature: Triumph took that rap.

Things were no more comfortable for the BSA group and the Brigadier. A string of unprofitable manoeuvres saw the share price tumble from £2.35 to 30p. The only reason he remained in the boardroom was because nobody on the factory floor trusted him with the spanners.

While all this was going on Triumph was paradoxically acquiring an iconic status in Hollywood, care of that chance late night call years earlier to Jo Mo. Steve McQueen may not have found anyone willing to insure him to jump the wire in *The Great Escape*, but in his own time there were no such restrictions. He was now a world class rider as well as the highest paid actor on the planet. This gave film directors sleepless nights particularly when he qualified to ride for the US Trials Team. Don Brown told the author:-

> *He got involved with the dealer we told him to go to in order to get service - Bud Ekins - they became great friends and Bud helped him to learn racing in the desert and he became rather good. Steve, Bud and I entered an enduro in northern California and we had great fun.*

There was nothing great about the management consultants the Brigadier used who now predicted that the vital American market, which had yielded the Queen's Award For Exports, would go into a slump. The short selling season of twelve weeks when both factories were frantically busy and piling the dollars sky high to keep them going would not be there. With that the Brigadier restructured everyone again and, as they were doing so, the American market actually boomed and broke sales records. Both Triumph and BSA had completely missed the selling season on which an entire year's profits depended. The only awards for exports that year went to Japan who built 85% of the motorcycles on American roads, which accounted for over a million units.

With that opportunity missed, fate presented the Brigadier with the chance to miss another. From his ranch in Colorado, bike nut and Gonzo journalist, Hunter S Thompson (he of *Fear And Loathing In Las Vegas* fame), applied to become a BSA dealer. He was no Steve McQueen but as an icon of the counter culture, an association with him would not have done any harm. The Brigadier could have taken the young apprentices off the factory floor to lunch and asked them what all this 'flower power' stuff was about. But that was unlikely in a motorcycle factory with an executive dining room in which Bert Hopwood had once been asked to remove his motorcycle jacket.

Whatever the Brigadier was planning next would require careful consideration, prudence and cunning. He would have to marshal all the wisdom he had acquired in the real world of hot metal industry. What would the 'financier of international renown' do next in what may be the final move for an entire industry that was vital to the British economy? Wait for it. He bought a country estate! (I am not making this up). Here amidst the peacocks and statues those 'born to lead' could divorce themselves from the grime of heavy industry and the uncouth who built motorcycles. Known universally as Mighty Marmalade Hall, its real name was the Group Research And Development Centre that was located at Umberslade Hall. When its annual upkeep of £1.5 million had been found, the Brigadier would have completely segregated design from production. If nothing else it would make a great commune for artists.

Mr Turner liked the finer things in life. Indeed his choice of hotels on the Gaffers' Gallop illustrates this, but the Brigadier had really upstaged him this time.

Mighty Marmalade Hall was described as a place of 'free form discussion groups' and let's not forget this was the sixties; Paris riots, pot smoking and all that. However the real talent stayed back at the factories.

Neale Shilton remained at Meriden and received bright young things who were designing motorcycles at Mighty Marmalade Hall without ever having visited a motorcycle factory. One day he was presented with a clay model of what petrol tanks would look like in the twenty first century. Neale recalled:-

> It seemed to me to have been inspired by a Grecian sculpture of a generously busted female, for the front of the tank was in the shape of two breasts which protruded like elongated headlamps...I told the young man that it was certainly imaginative, but useless as it was sometimes necessary for a motorcycle to go round a corner. He was very upset having wasted weeks of work. He had simply been told to design a tank and nothing had been said about front forks.

All this gave their rivals the breathing space to shake the earth. Whilst Bert Hopwood looked out of his window he knew, as did Mr Soichiro Honda, that markets existed, not in the heads of consultants but beyond the factory gates in the heads of consumers. He had disagreed with Mr Turner himself over motorcycle design. Two cylinders were not enough and this was the final significant decision that Mr Turner frankly got wrong. Bert wanted to produce a three cylinder motorcycle by simply adding an extra cylinder to Mr Turner's own Speed Twin. It was a simple and highly effective stop gap. Then Bert would work on modernising a modular range, which was based on several sizes with common parts: industry standard practice today.

Mr Turner and Bert Hopwood did not have the best of relations and perhaps Mr Turner knew that Bert was a serious rival for whom, had he the 'gift of the gab' and Jack Sangster's patronage, this may be a very different story. Finally, in 1965 the factory produced a superb prototype. By then Mr Turner had retired, but still exercised influence and pressured the Brigadier to resist in favour of a more modern design that he was developing, known as the Bandit. Triumph hesitated, engaged consultants and later the Brigadier heard a rumour that would put him on national television. At one of the many meetings, the Brigadier held court until the end when they were on their feet and the point was made:-

> *Oh by the way, I learned today that Honda will shortly be marketing a 750cc machine.*

It was like a punch in the stomach to the Brigadier who brought everyone back to their seats rather sharply. By now the media had noticed how badly run the motorcycle industry had become whilst simultaneously failing to see Honda coming. The TV news and documentary makers wanted to hear from the Brigadier himself. His place in history is a black and white newsreel in which he sits in one of the nation's drawing rooms, reality and its camera crew having invaded his oak panelled sanctuary. Wider at the waist and fatter at the jowls after years of good living off the industry he did not care for, the Brigadier fielded the question, how had he failed to see the Japanese coming?

> *Absolutely wrong yes, ill-informed comment. We have known for some time that the Japanese would be coming into the bigger market...anybody that comes in new is bound to* NIBBLE AWAY A LITTLE BIT *(author's emphasis).*

I guess Honda were more peckish than he realised....

He could have spared himself the discomfort had he opened the big desk draw at which Mr Turner used to sit and read his report on the Japanese industry. Mr Turner opened:-

> *The revelations of Japan as a whole are truly shocking...Japan has ninety million highly energetic, purposeful people all geared to an economic machine with the avowed object of becoming great again.*

And as if designed for the Brigadier's very own ears:-

It is essential that our industry in general and the BSA group in particular should know the facts and what we are up against in the retention of our export markets.

Mr Turner gave him ten years notice!

Britain was on the verge of becoming the first and only advanced nation on earth to acquire the notion that an economy can run without a manufacturing base. As she did so the second most powerful nation on earth delivered the Honda 750-4, a four cylinder superbike. Electric start and indicators had arrived and Honda had reinvented the motorcyclist from hard man of the open road into the consumer who did not bother with spanners. Historians point to this as the moment in history when the British motorcycle industry finally died, but they are not entirely right. Despite bizarre management methods and poor labour relations Triumph would hit the circuits, free of Mr Turner's caution against racing, and win a string of victories that would leave its rivals standing. All this was down to a handful of unsung heroes, devoted to Triumph and operating in old factories on tight budgets. For a brief moment it would feel like the fine old factory was at last allowed to deliver its full potential.

Meanwhile the youth of the era were rioting in Grosvenor Square over the Vietnam War. Those that went to university were starting to eschew engineering in favour of sociology and documentary makers became self-indulgent and tried to leave the illusion that 'if you can remember the sixties, you weren't there.' Not surprisingly, many were not.

Back at the factory, Mr Turner's own 1936 designed Speed Twin grew into a 750cc triple by the addition of an extra cylinder. Whilst consumer magazines raved about the Honda's indicators and comfort, Triumph finally produced the Trident in 1969 that they could have brought out in 1965. In terms of speed and handling, if not refinement, it left the Honda behind and would take the Production World Championship titles well into the next decade. This was down to the studied intensity of the designer, Doug Hele and his unusually short tester with an over developed sense of humour, Percy Tait. With money painfully tight, Percy and Doug had to sneak out on public roads for their high speed testing. Doug would lie in the verge and observe as Percy wound back the prototype's throttle to speeds that the Honda 'nicer people' 750 had never achieved. Percy recalls,

I came along at a fair old speed and as she was laid over these bumps she began to hop about a bit. The buggers were lying in the grass in my line of fire and they all got into the ditch when they saw me coming. Must have done old Doug's bowels a lot of good.

Not quite the meticulous regimented tests of Japan's mightiest.

By the 1970s the brush that painted the broad sweep of history seemed to have lost its bristles. We joined the Common Market, Cliff Richard entered the Eurovision Song Contest and the Royal Navy went into battle over an unattractive North Sea fish. The Cod War with Iceland preceded an invasion of the Colorado potato beetle and the nation's fish and chips were in peril. We could not seem to get anything right and when we felt it couldn't get any worse, kipper ties became fashionable. It was simply a naff decade but Momma always told me that I should be more tolerant of other people's opinions. Maybe, but always bear in mind that the 1960s gave us Jimi Hendrix and the 1970s Jimmy Osmond. It's a no brainer.

Meanwhile, in the cold reality of the Triumph factory, Doug Hele had concerns about his young draughtsman Norman Hyde. Young men become devoted to motorcycles and Norman was designing them all week and racing them all weekend. Norman had no idea where his efforts would lead them but his creations included parts made for hitherto unachieved speeds. One of those included a titanium rocker (part of an engine as opposed to a Mod basher), which he showed to his boss. Doug did a quick pound/foot calculation in his head, called for a hammer, hit the rocker arm in the right spot and made it crack. Today, committees would sit for a fortnight around a computer screen with a 3D image to test the strength of parts and then still get it wrong. However, Norman got it right when it really counted.

By now it was clear that the era of *La Dolce Vita* was over and the summer breeze was a health and safety issue. Jealous bald bureaucrats turned their gaze to the better coiffured and insisted that hairy bikers kept their flowing locks a secret by making crash helmets compulsory. Of this Mr Turner would not have approved, for he habitually rode helmetless and only reluctantly donned one for the Gaffer's Gallop to protect him from the weather. That freedom to choose was wrested from the individual by those who knew better. They had found their appetite for compulsion and once tasted they never forgot.

Back on the track Triumph were Production World Champions year in and year out. The famous Triumph triumvirate of Hopwood, Hele and designer Brian Jones were the best in the world at that time. Their achievements came about because they simply wanted to build motorcycles and they were never to receive the recognition they deserved. Britain as a nation was changing and soon young Turks would admire asset strippers, even elevating them to parliament, rather than inventors who were dismissed with the curious notion that industry was a byword for backwardness. Moving with the times was in turn a euphemism for being unsentimental, rude and even corrupt. From now on business was about show rather then substance. Norman Hyde would pay tribute to Doug Hele's opposing approach, at his funeral years later:-

All business was done with a shake of the hand – a gentleman's way of doing business. Doug worked 24 hours a day without any shouting or arm waving. He had a wonderful ability to extract the best from people. He cared about people.

Arguably his greatest achievement came on the 24th of September, 1972 on the Concorde runway at Fairford. A band of hairy Midlanders wheeled out of their tired transit van the fastest motorcycle and racing sidecar on earth. This was a Trident built and ridden by Norman: the Hyde Roadrunner. It was a morning not unlike that a few years previously when fellow Triumph rider Donald Campbell lowered himself into the cockpit of the Bluebird on Coniston Water. In both cases a solitary aerodynamic dart would streak across a flat landscape with their engines at full cry. Norman was on his way to taking the World Speed Record. The Trident's sound was ghostly with its roots firmly in Mr Turner's 1936 Speed Twin. Three cylinders were flat out and on their way to a world record: the final testament. Respect! (As they say these days).

Meanwhile the Brigadier had been replaced by, amongst others, a former fighter ace. Dennis 'Biggles' Poore DFC came from a motor sport background, was a right wing Tory, Lloyd's name and had friends in high places. The industry was in such a state that he did not have time to mince his words and one day in 1974, the workers read a headline on the billboard of the *Coventry Telegraph* announcing that their factory would close. The order went out, 'call a meeting and get a chain' which was promptly wrapped around Triumph's famous factory gates and the padlock snapped firmly shut. The workers were prepared to sit it out for as long as it took. It would be a long time before any new Triumphs hit the road again, and thus began the famous blockade. Ironically, Mighty Marmalade Hall enjoyed its most productive week when the swans on the lake produced two cygnets.

It was 1974 and the Japanese soldier, Hoyoo Oonda, emerged from the jungle having finally been persuaded that the Second World War had come to an end whereas Lord Lucan, by contrast, disappeared. The dock workers went on strike, the railway men, car workers and coal miners were poised and ready to spring. The country looked increasingly unstable and there was a fuel shortage during which my wife's budgie died. It was as well that Mr Turner did not have to witness this, although he would have been unmoved by the loss of a budgie.

Back on the Gaffer's Gallop in 1953, Mr Turner had done all that was humanly possible to secure Triumph's future. The foregoing account of Triumph after Mr Turner would have been viewed as the product of a mind set on a train of thought whilst immersed in narcotics or too much gin and tonic, as was rather more fashionable at the time. Thus as Mr Turner rode on in the autumn calm of the second Elizabethan age the populace were yet to be treated to Jimi Hendrix, the Common Market or the prospect of postage stamps devoid of Her Majesty's head. The world went about its business as Mr Turner happily made use of the web of roads that had been thrown up around these once feudal lands. These served the massed legions of workers making the industrial Midlands the workshop of the world. The new Knights of the Round Table were the industrialists and Mr Turner, in my unbiased view, a pretty good candidate for its King Arthur. His road map bore the signs of his forebears, crossed swords denoted many an ancient battlefield including Bosworth and Lucton. Yet it was the Grand Union Canal, subsequently overtaken by the railroad, and finally the road itself, that scarred the landscape now. Here old wealth, bearing the patina of age stood aloof as the tide of the eager and the hurried came in without time for deference before they were finally engulfed leaving only the occasional outcrop.

The Gaffers wound back their throttles and made their way through the traffic. Small engines warm up quickly and to the Gaffers' delight they soon left their car bound companions behind.

They followed the course of the Grand Union Canal by which time they were roughly level with Umberslade Hall, one of the increasingly rare outcrops of old money. As one whose temper was too short and suits too sharp, Mr Turner was the embodiment of the newly rich. After dinner cigars and shooting aside, he did not care. He lived in the real world and in the unlikely event that he gave Umberslade a thought it would have been as a consequence of the bond that binds mariners. For in 1941, Lieutenant Sir Gerard Philip Graves Muntz and his submarine went to the seabed taking with them the last Baronetcy of Umberslade that had initially been created in the 12th century by Henry II. Like the Old Bell at Malmesbury, Umberslade had its fair share of High Sheriffs and Deputy Lieutenants. From crusaders and mercenaries descended those who manned the final phase of Empire. They bore the unshakable belief that the sun would never set upon their Imperial ideal and their duty was to spread literacy, the rule of law and Christianity from 'this sceptred Isle' to 'less happier lands'. Whilst much maligned today, the British Empire actually had other nations petition the throne to enjoy the benefits of all that went with British rule including justice, gunboats, *Carry On* films, Earl Grey tea and cucumber sandwiches. To maintain this, the issue of the great houses were brutalised by boarding schools to toughen them up in a way that one would not dare to treat a galley slave. The 'cream' turned their backs on commerce and the life of the landed to serve, often in the Imperial Service. The Empire depended on it and called upon those from 'the upper middle classes, stamped to a pattern by English public schools and the ancient universities' to maintain Pax Britannica. From there one descended into the ranks of the law, the clergy, the army and if all else failed, politics. One had a duty to future generations and the Empire. It is quaint but it served us well. Then came the Battle of the Somme and the seeds of its destruction were well and truly sown. By the Second World War, mothers once again gave up their sons so their grandsons would be free but the ultimate sacrifice was never to be taken for granted again. The loss of Lieutenant Muntz at sea and that of many young men and women from homes grand and humble across the Kingdom secured the future of the post war generation and the freedom to pass on their legacy. Having been charged to 'export or die', Mr Turner invested that legacy in the former. He knew that as the last shot was fired in the Second World War, so was the opening shot in the ensuing economic battle. Parliament's answer was to treat the manufacturing sector as if it lowered the tone of the neighbourhood. Like Mighty Marmalade Hall, you couldn't make it up.

The rumble of passing motorcycles did not permeate that significant stately pile. Umberslade Hall was a proper 17th century country mansion, set in its own grounds, the lucky incumbents having once enjoyed the services of 30 members of staff, vast acres, and an art collection. It was quite deliberately remote from the daily grind of making money because by the time you were at Umberslade that money had been made and its daily management was a job in itself. A more unsuitable place for the motorcycle industry it is impossible to conceive and as Mr Turner rode by he would certainly have agreed in the highly unlikely event that such a strange notion ever crept into his thoughts.

Even though Mr Turner appreciated art he would not make the connection between Umberslade's 17th century marble sculpture of *The Crouching Venus* by John Van Nost the Elder. It depicts Venus on being surprised just after bathing and crouching as she covers her ample breasts. It was a grand sight to greet young motorcycle designers as they stepped into the hall each morning. Venus's breasts appear to have played on the imagination of the graduate on whom the task of designing a new petrol tank fell.

Had anyone tried telling the Gaffers in 1953 that their mighty industry would come to this they may have secured employment as a court jester. Mr Turner was currently more concerned with proving to Britons only just emerging from an age of austerity, that he could make a gallon of their hard earned petrol transport them for over 100 miles. Thus to Mr Turner, Meriden and the industrial Midlands stood for one thing and one thing only as far as he was concerned: profit. When I passed the same way fifty four years later it was all about sentiment and powerful sentiment at that.

OUR INDUSTRIAL DUNKIRK

Dawn seemed to break early as a brief shaft of sunlight lit up my tent, pitched somewhere to the south of Leamington Spa. I stumbled out and was brought to by a man in brogues and twill trousers looking at me out of the corner of his eye and exclaiming, "The cricket news is that Long Itchington have won by eleven runs."

And with that he paced away to the big house with his spaniel at his heels. I scratched my head, pulled my soap bag out of the panniers and made for that period toilet block whilst being serenaded by a song thrush above my tent. Mr Turner may have spent his night in the splendour of the Regent Hotel but I would not have swapped with him.

On my return I spotted a father and son as they paused by the Triumph and Dad pointed to the large chrome mouth organ tank badge, an unmistakable bequest from the 1950s.

"It looks brand new."

"It very nearly is."

He looked quizzically at the back and front of the bike and added a little doubtfully, "I didn't know they made them anymore."

"It's a long story."

Shortly I rode through the avenue of trees stirred by the morning breeze and back on to the road. The prospect of seeing Meriden in the flesh has never been dampened by the oft spoken words, 'there's nothing there mate'. However there is. There is a story that has to be told.

I rode on until I came to the nearest petrol station and filled her up where a new accent greeted me. Then it was on to Leamington Spa, land of wide lawns and afternoon tea. Leamington still had the feel of some distant colonial capital under blue skies with a relaxed ambience. It was everything that Stratford was not: friendly.

I turned the corner at the bottom of the hill, passing the town hall and the statue of Queen Victoria. Heading up the hill, the sun caught the bright front of a magnificent regency building. Was it a sign? At no point in this journey was there any event, coincidence or something faintly strange that even with a truck load of literary license would add a much needed spooky twist to this tale. Up until now, the door to Mr Turner's celestial office remained firmly closed. However this rare break in the clouds did cause the sun to fall on the appropriately named Regent Hotel, but then that probably happens every morning at this time.

I duly swung the Triumph around in the road and pulled up between the Grecian columns. All was quiet as the incumbent reps had departed to dispense their industrial plastics and insurance policies on the unsuspecting. I put the bike on the side stand and strolled up the well worn steps under the coat of arms. There, through the swing doors was the foyer in which the Gaffers and their entourage had assembled on the morning of Wednesday the 7th of October, 1953. The place now looked like it had become the victim of cheap breaks that came with tabloid newspapers. The skirting board was scuffed by luggage on wheels and the foyer silent as all hands were clearing away the breakfast plates. The echo of Mr Tuner that had once dissipated up there under the high ceiling was long gone.

I parked the Triumph down by the statue of Queen Victoria and had a quick look at the town. Relaxed, multicultural, spacious and best of all no incomprehensible modern architecture. Or perhaps this was just the effect of the sunshine.

An elderly gentleman pushed his wife in a wheel-chair in front of the bike. He too was pointing at the badge on the tank. He was either out of breath or his wife was genuinely interested in motorcycle tank badges. Either way the time had come for me to make my way to Meriden and all that poignantly happened there at a pivotal point in British history.

I left Leamington as my mind's eye replayed the newsreels from a generation ago and I recalled all that I had read about a very human place from where the workers took on the world. It really could not happen today but once upon a time people were confident that they could change things and cared enough to try.

I increased the silky smooth speed of my new Triumph, before my thoughts returned to the 1970s. For in 'those days' it was not a good time to be in the motorcycle industry. The Department of Trade and Industry was, incredibly, being run by someone who had an open aversion to motorcycles, much to the delight of our competitors. Peter Walker was described by Britain's satirical magazine, *Private Eye* as "...an unscrupulous smarmy faced arrogant little con man". Peter was the Walker formerly of Slater Walker asset strippers and an appropriate appointee if you hold the view that Charles Manson was good for family values. If Peter had any empathy with Triumph's difficulties given those experienced by Slater Walker when they rocked the City amidst scandal, he did not show it. Meanwhile one of our biggest export earners was allowed to continue withering on the vine until the happy arrival of the nation's favourite socialist, none other than 'Wedgie The Whizz' himself, Tony Benn.

By now Meriden was making the headlines in a largely sympathetic press. The nation's foremost motorcycle pressure group, the Motorcycle Action Group, arranged a 'Save Meriden' rally. The resolve of the workers hardened prompting Biggles to comment that, 'we didn't bargain for the strength of their reaction'. He made but one visit to the factory and could not help but notice that which is missing today; pride of place. People at Meriden liked what they did, followed their parents there, got married there and one elderly worker ultimately had his ashes spread on the lawn in front of the factory. This was a feeling that had nothing to do with moronic management and truculent trade unions. This was about people and prompted a *Sunday Times* profile to refer to Meriden as 'a drama...of central importance to British industrial history'.

Meanwhile Biggles was onto the worker's tail (he would, in the style of the school boy hero refer to them as Bandits) and made them all redundant. They took their money and went back to the warmth of their brazier, marginally better off but no further forward.

The ensuing stand off was more than metaphorical. As the weeks rolled by, a secret meeting was arranged at a hotel near Heathrow. Biggles and a Bandit sat and stared at each other and could not even agree on who should buy the tea. Unlike the notorious unions of the day, particularly the miners who were indifferent to viability, the Bandits believed Triumph should remain in business precisely because they were viable. If the management had not got the nerve, the workers had and would run the factory as a co-operative. Wedgie was interested, parliament was not.

Biggles had another go at the Bandits by threatening to retrieve his assets from the factory. The Bandits then revealed that they had 4,000 supporters whom they could coach in, within the hour, to stand guard 24/7. Biggles had never had a 'dog fight' quite like this one.

The Prime Minister, Harold Wilson, also had problems. Meriden was not his prime concern. Neither were the miners, the car workers nor the dockers. His own intelligence services had him labelled an 'untrustworthy bastard' and in the final rear guard action of the old establishment, were rumoured to be seeking to oust him, incredibly by means of a military coup! Now in Britain we do picnics well, whereas Latin Americans are naturals when it comes to trouble on the streets. But this quiet nation of old guards in bowler hats had had enough. The industrial unrest and an economy facing 'whole scale domestic liquidation' was not the reason why some had endured the North Atlantic Convoy or even Dad's Army.

Harold stood nervously behind the sash windows of his Westminster flat. It was a short rumble for the tanks from Horse Guards to the Houses of Parliament and he realised that London has at its heart the military establishment. Behind the anonymous brass plated door of the Special Forces Club in Herbert Crescent, Knightsbridge and all the way up to Buckingham Palace, the old establishment could be seen but not heard. To make matters worse, Harold's mates were a bit dodgy and dreary which contrasted with the raffish 'chaps' of the capital's gentlemen's clubs particularly the aristocratic Clermont. Harold's mates included John Stonehouse MP; the unluckiest philanderer on earth who left his clothes on the beach and made out that he had 'done a Reggie Perrin'. Unfortunately for the randy MP this coincided with the disappearance of the Clermont's Lord Lucan. It was a bad time to even faintly resemble the naughty Earl and a 'Lucan spotting' craze spread across the Commonwealth. As randy John passed through Australian customs, the officers thought they would brighten up their day by pouncing on the first Englishman of that certain haughty bearing just in case it turned out to be the equally unlucky Earl. Their consolation prize was not a landed toff but a much sought after former Minister of Aviation, who rather than having been swallowed up by the waves in a most dramatic adieu, actually left behind his wife and assorted political worries and eloped to Australia with his secretary.

Cabinet ministers were disappearing, the economy was out of control and the Judiciary were still being made to feel like man-servants to the aristocracy. It turned out that the inappropriately named Lord 'Lucky' Lucan had been home to murder his estranged wife and tragically got his children's nanny instead. A trial ensued in his absence that had to be stopped as the key witnesses had to dash off on compassionate grounds. Alas they turned up on the front page of the papers, having been photographed at Ascot and close to the Royal Box at that!

One way or another Harold seemed to have taken on a grey veneer, not helped by having a cabinet of bespectacled blokes in ill-fitting suits, all of whom seemed to be called Roy. Contrast this with the sharp suited Clermont owner and icon of fading Imperial values, John 'Aspers' Aspinall. Aspers had the veneer of an aristocratic villain, the brain of a scholar and once famously proclaimed that he would rather trust the safety of his grandchildren to gorillas than social workers. When the media tired of reporting on Harold's under performing government their attention would be drawn to Lucan's mates. Asper's life of notoriety was about to begin by speaking of the Lucan trial and exclaiming that one should be loyal to one's friends (and class) over and above the oath to the Court. It was no longer clear who was running the country but either way they were crazy guys, one and all.

Harold could scarcely have picked a worse time in history to be in power and the Bandits could not have picked a worse time to man the pickets, for it snowed. Biggles then switched off the electricity and water supply at which point the factory's internal sewage system stopped working and waste emerged through the ground. It was now all down to Morecambe and Wise to deliver the ultimate Christmas show to lift the nation's spirits.

The brazier at Triumph's famous factory gates burned on into the long cold nights as Biggles repaired to his London club to let the winter winds from Russia do their worst. It felt like a long time since the Gaffers had swept through those gates and onto the Gallop. Along the fence at the front of the factory that they had once passed at speed, read the sign to passing traffic:-

Remember, Triumph Stays At Meriden Where The Legend Was Made

Beside this was a shelter erected from wood and plastic and an assortment of canteen chairs. Soon the Bandits became the stars of the BBC *Man Alive* documentary special entitled *For The Love Of Triumph*. Those that could afford a television set could see themselves on the silver screen. This did not please everyone and one of Biggles right hand men, the 'Pink Panther' (known as such for his customary gait) accused the BBC of bias.

When not being minor celebrities the Bandits played dominoes, their wives manned the tea urn and provided free meals from the canteen. They also read their own newssheet produced by this embattled community that was fighting for Mr Turner's 'little factory in England'. As they did all this they kept their factory as clean as possible, checked stocks and serviced production machinery, but it was hard for the family men in their midst. They knew that at school other children would ask theirs, "what did you get for Christmas?" The children of Meriden would go without that year, yet before the Thatcher/Blair era of the glorious self above all else, the strength of community showed its mettle. The wives and children of Meriden had stood by their men. The days were short, the puddles deep and the wind blew as the worker's families passed through the factory gates for the children's Christmas party. This was held in the factory canteen with Santa Claus being played by a Union convenor. It was the best they could do that year and it would have been far easier to give in and pick up their acrylic uniform from the local supermarket. But then there would have been no Triumph in the millennium and, importantly for the new breed of fast talking politicians, no huge exports from the very last of British industry. Of somewhat less importance, I would not be making this journey.

I rode down the A45 as the traffic thickened and ground to a standstill. On the old A45, Mr Turner had leaped from his office in his sharpest suit, picked up a bike off the production line and wound back the throttle to 100mph: from boardroom to the ton in a matter of minutes. And before rolling roads teams of testers flew down the road every half hour or so. The Metropolitan Police and the White Helmets motorcycle display team had passed having picked up scores of Triumphs. Legends were made but not on this road, for Meriden has since been bypassed. It could have been anywhere, not least as we were all stuck in a traffic jam.

From Pasadena, California to Woodside, New York, dealers scratched their heads and wondered why in the little island of the King and Queen and village green they could not organise themselves to supply a product that Mr Turner had ensured would remain in demand. Well they might, as many dealers in the US could recall the era when British bikes outnumbered Harley Davidson four to one in their own country. They were tempted by the view that modern Britain was an unworthy heir to a glorious heritage. Be that as it may, or may not be, the Bandits sought to restore Triumph to its former glories. They went to America where perplexed dealers confirmed the demand for their impounded legend. Consequently a business plan was prepared and the government duly petitioned. Meanwhile at Meriden the electricity bill was now being paid by wage contributions from other Trade Unions in the Coventry area following Biggles' move to have it cut off.

The battle dragged on with wives having to go out to work as two wage families and latch door children were a rarity then. Support remained but numbers dwindled on the back of a promise that jobs would be restored when the worker's Co-operative was established. It was something to look forward to. Gone would be the practice of 'Meriden Monday' when the staff got splashed by passing chauffeurs coming to pick up their hard earned money to keep Jolly, the Brigadier and assorted hangers on in a country estate at Mighty Marmalade Hall. Gone also would be trade union restrictive practices and strikes called by bully boy shop stewards. Worker democracy was in and there was no remote management to kick against: it would be like kicking against themselves. All would have the same rate of pay whether in the office or on the factory floor. It would be utopia. Word came from Wedgie that he was in favour (bless him). The sight of trades unions wanting to work rather than stopping others from working was in sharp contrast to the antics employed in other disputes that were in the news.

Donations from well-wishers amongst the public flooded in but Biggles was not giving up. He came in for one last attack at the Bandits and applied for an injunction to release the assets, which as owner of Triumph he viewed as his all along anyway. Wedgie got word and followed on his tail with a promise to peel off if he did not fill the lawyers pockets. In return Wedgie would use his personal influence and get the blockade lifted, which he duly did when it dawned on Biggles that the world had changed since 'so much was owed by so many to so few'.

It was a new dawn and the chattering classes briefly turned their attention to a motorcycle factory. That factory even made it onto the West End stage with a piece of agitprop theatre which then went on national tour. It went by the catchy title of, *Events Following The Closure Of A Motorcycle Factory*.

Behind the picket lines was the incongruous sight of motorcycles being tested up and down the car park. Tester Chuck Knight rode eleven thousand miles and carried out over ninety three thousand gear changes during the blockade. All this took place without pay to ensure that the new design worked when the bikes started rolling again. Draughtsman Frank Thompson, who had been at the factory since 1947, carried out this design work as the Triumph name meant a lot to these guys.

I untangled myself from the traffic, took the roundabout by the art deco hotel close to Coventry Airport into which Triumph's land speed record bikes had been flown from America. However I was not flying anywhere as I now retraced my steps up the carriageway from whence I had come. Finally I made it to the Meriden roundabout and turned onto the long straight leading to the geographical centre of England. An old barn on my right had been converted into a health farm and golfers in polo necks on my left hauled their trolleys across the green. Had it all really happened here?

Even with Wedgie's favour the Co-op's creation was by no means guaranteed. Faith has no feature on the balance sheet but Wedgie's faith led to the despatch of an accountant from his department to help the workers prepare a business plan. Significantly, local MP and future Paymaster General, Geoffrey Robinson added professionalism to what would shortly become a fledgling business.

Now Wedgie and the workers found themselves up against both the left and right wing establishments. He would record that even within the civil service:-

> I could have moved much more quickly if I had not found it so difficult with my officials and the hostility of the establishment. What really frightened the establishment was that the ultimate discipline of private ownership was the sack and if people could escape it by sit ins and then establishing Co-ops it undermined the whole basis of industrial discipline.

Biggles and the Bandits had parted mid-dogfight while Wedgie had the unenviable task of dealing with his civil servants.

Finally the Bandits ended up paying Biggles £4.9 million of public money for the Triumph factory after he had set out looking for £7.3 million. Better still, a debate was only necessary in Parliament if over £5 million of public money was required. Wedgie could therefore stick two fingers up at the trades union toadies on the Labour benches and the massed ranks of asset strippers on the Conservative benches. And that is why he is the nation's favourite socialist.

The dream was born but the nightmare would follow. The government eventually loaned the workers £4.95m and promptly took £200k for their own 'accountancy services'. All the bikes had to be marketed through Biggles, a man hardly well disposed to the Workers' Co-operative. Interest rates would cripple them and leave nothing for the much needed reinvestment in plant and new models that the competition would bring out annually. Geoffrey Robinson would describe the deal as being like:-

> Rescuing a drowning man in the middle of a lake and leaving him up to his neck in quicksand.

Robinson told the workers not to accept, but they were motorcycle engineers. This high-risk poker is the natural fare of politicians and businessmen whereas family men simply want next Christmas to be their children's best and with that they took the offer. Just in the nick of time as it happened as Wedgie was replaced and in his department there appeared a report from the Boston Consulting Group (known as the Boston Stranglers) which condemned the British motorcycle industry as a whole. That industry was now on its own, and the ruling Labour party started its slow withdrawal from the industrial matters of its grimy benefactors, curiously without a corresponding reduction in the size of the civil service. Dealing with striking school teachers and single issue fanatics would shape the party's future and lead to the election of a Prime Minister who could not tell the difference between a minaret and a missile. Wedgie would always be a thorn in the side of the post socialist Labour Party and evolve into a national institution in his own right.

In a cold factory in Meriden on Monday the 10th of March, 1975 the lights came on, the heating was cranked up and bikes started to roll off the production line. All were on a flat salary of £50 per week except Geoffrey Robinson who gave his time and ample talents for free. The older workers came back through the factory gates on the promise of 'a job for life' and the shop steward Dennis Johnson, a man committed to industrial democracy, was in at 7 am and encouraged worker participation in all decisions by holding mass meetings on a Saturday morning so as to avoid disruption to production. It was a million miles from the rest of strike-ridden Britain.

The 'Billy big talk' accountancy system of the Brigadier proved inoperable and a Miss Brenda Price, who had worked under Mr Turner, restored the one used by him. A young leader by the name of John Rosamund was appointed as chairman of the Workers' Board of Directors. John was a big affable welder who was uncomfortable with the limelight and promptly sent Brenda to America to check out the markets there. I know that on TV heroes do not answer to names like Brenda or John, but these were real people from an age before we turned into a nation obsessed with celebrity and image. Having said that Brenda was quite a looker, between you and I.

John would also see off Richard and Mopsa English who would circumnavigate the globe on a donated Triumph and publish their book *Full Circle* on their return. They were photographed on their departure at the front of the factory under the Triumph logo and the usual array of reinstalled Union Jacks that had witnessed the Gaffers' Gallop. Other travellers included university lecturer Paul Pratt who stayed out on his Triumph for fifteen years and published *World Understanding On Two Wheels*. However the most significant journey was that undertaken by author Ted Simon just before the blockade. Ted went on to publish *Jupiter's Travels*, a book widely regarded as one of the best travel books of all time and the inspiration behind Ewan and Charlie's *Long Way Round*.

The very first of the Co-op's bikes only hit the streets by accident. They first of all had to pass the noise regulations and curiously one of the Co-op's biggest detractors, Biggles was hanging around during the tests. To his delight the noisy old Bonneville failed. However Doug Hele, who was by then in his employment, was also present and pointed out to the workers that something was loose. This was promptly tightened and the bike passed the test much to Biggles annoyance. God bless you Doug.

The workers felt they had a debt to pay and sent their very first bike to the singer David Essex who had been a vocal supporter through their darkest hour. He picked up the bike in a blaze of publicity with his mate, Formula 1 World Champion, James Hunt in tow. Triumph were back in town.

Interest payments and a permanent cash shortage preventing essential reinvestment did not stop the workforce generating a small profit by 1976. It could succeed, but Meriden is a long way from the well insulated life of the nation's political elite in Westminster and the Prime Minister, Harold Wilson had more on his plate. He heard that tanks had turned up at Heathrow airport and was advised that he could not count on the military to protect him if the mercenaries that were alleged to have assembled at assorted country estates, launched a coup. Worse still, the last Viceroy of India, Lord Louis Mountbatten of Burma, was allegedly poised to replace him. His speech to Parliament had already been prepared and was rumoured to be circulating within the confines of Buck House. Now in Latin America, the streets would have burned, in Italy the trains would have run on time and even the French would have given in to the temptation to chuck a brick or two. But this was Britain, the social season came around and everyone went to the horse races. Not a lot of blood was spilt but a great deal of strawberries and cream were devoured in London. 'Up North' it was a different story.

A coup is a good reason to resign in any other country in the world, except dear old Blighty. Alas we only have scandals over sex and the Prime Minister was about to fire his parting shot. Rumours had long been circulating that Harold had been knocking his pipe out on the bedside table of his private secretary, Marcia Williams. He now bestowed on her a title, which attracted the merciless attention of *Private Eye*. Under the headline 'Its Lady Slagheap' we see round-shouldered Harold gazing into Marcia's eyes while his speech bubble reads,

"So Marcia, I've made a Lady of you at last"
"Ooh saucy" she replies.

A long way from Meriden, Wedgie's unsympathetic successor could not help but notice that this curious Co-operative beyond Westminster was surviving. Indeed it was producing the biggest selling 750cc in Britain. The Bonneville mopped up 32 percent of all sales right from under the nose of its old foe, the Honda 750-4. The promise of meeting 'nicer people on a Honda' was not enough and so Honda dropped their price and held it artificially low in the hope that the embattled old vessel of Meriden would slip below the surface and Japan would rule the waves. In this they failed, despite the Co-op's marketing arm that was still being run by Biggles, refusing to match Honda's price.

Back in the factory, it was all hands on deck. That famous Triumph quality of deep lustered paint and thick chrome was being maintained as its distinctive feature in an increasingly plastic market place. The tanks had their coach lines painted by hand by men who had been pulled out of retirement. Around thirty percent of the entire workforce had been there since before the war and on passing through the factory they could remember the figure of Mr Turner walking down their very production line, the glory days of world speed records and Steve McQueen's visits. Now they saw a leaking roof over their factory in which only half of the floor space was occupied. The machinery was clapped out from when the Meriden staff were thrashed by the export drive of the Brigadier and Harry Sturgeon. They had simply taken the money and failed to reinvest and this was their legacy. The worker's legacy was their skill that ensured that Triumphs continued to roll off the production line and be the star of any showroom that they graced with their presence. To a youthful Geoffrey Robinson, British products sold on heritage and he compared the Triumph to the MGB, both of which were traditionally made and gradually improved by evolution. Well, it worked with mankind.

With the government tied up in problems of its own making, the Meriden vessel was adrift at sea and needed a seasoned captain. The Co-operative was still working on the sincere belief in industrial democracy based on trust, hard work, honesty, full sick pay, no clocking on or off with all staff enjoying the same privileges, regardless of rank. And for a time it worked. But with an ambivalent government wrestling with a striking public sector and Honda holding it's price down from $2,100 to $1,600, change was inevitable. At this point the former works manager who gave forty years of his life to Triumph, John Nelson, returned. Cambridge alumnus or not he wasted no time in shaking the hand of every one of the 700 workers at the factory. Incredibly the factory started to feel like it had under Mr Turner's highly successful tenure.

The workers went on to tenaciously face one crisis after another and time and again the question resonated around the echoing factory, 'what would Mr Turner have done?' The same question was being asked over a decade after his death.

Slowly, worker democracy gave way to harsh reality and the need, as one worker told John Nelson, for a 'real bastard in here'. Geoffrey Robinson became the still unpaid Chief Executive and although ascendant in the government he had no power to cancel the debt around the Co-op's neck; a concession given to far more expensive and less successful government assisted enterprises of the day.

At this point Margaret Thatcher swept to power in a 3½ litre Rover equipped with a poem about Francis Assisi and a contract on the head of the President of the National Union of Mine Workers. She lost the Rover, got the President and for better or worse Britain would never be the same again.

Stormy seas were ahead for the battle scarred vessel Meriden, which were uncomfortable when the water level was only just being kept below the bow. None of these were of the workers' making and their factory was more like a family business whose customers preferred a motorcycle that was so well made it could pass from one generation to the next. Still the stricken vessel cut its path through currency fluctuations, interest rates and inflation, all of which took their toll. They had to consider the unthinkable; job losses, everything that the Co-operative stood against. But this advice came from the man who gave his time for free, Geoffrey Robinson. In him they trusted.

The first cut was the hardest: the blockade veterans over sixty-five. The very men who had come back because their skills were needed to compensate for the worn out machinery. One told the press:-

> I have been treated as if I was just an employee of any private company and not as a member of a workers cooperative.

It was no easy task to place the palm of one's hand on the shoulder of a proud old craftsman and tell him to gather his tools.

The public, being the public, dug deep and thousands of pounds of donations rolled in; this was a business like no other. Consequently my journey down the tree lined road leading to Meriden was tinged with emotion. Much maligned today, it plays no part in making money but can be an overriding factor in making a purchase. If only purchasers would be logical, the world could be bland and markets divided up between a few producers who would be masters of the universe.

I eased up alongside the village sign that read:-

> Meriden, the centre of England

It had been stormy the previous night and there were branches and debris in the road. Hard hat Hi-Viz types took their chain saws to the odd branch before throwing them in the back of a Land Rover. No one was in a hurry and they only broke the silence occasionally. They went about their business oblivious to my presence as the clouds parted and sunlight fell upon the lush green roadside. Time has clearly moved on.

As 1980 came around, thousands of motorcyclists gathered at Meriden. On this road they had rumbled by before riding all the way to Downing Street to implore that Triumph be saved, whilst the public cheered from this very verge. That emotion can be a powerful thing.

It was not the throbbing of thousands of Triumphs outside the Prime Minister's pad that lead to a cancellation of the government debt. It was the belief that they had no chance of getting it back, so what the hell. They could have done it a bit sooner but Westminster is a long way from Britain and governments only care when they are up for election. The cancellation did not clear all the debts by any means and the local authority came round for their cut of the rates as with any other business.

The workmen moved the 'Tree Cutting In Progress' sign further down the road and broke for tea. They were too young to have attended the Meriden factory's Family Christmas Party.

In March 1982, John Rosamund had pulled the corner of a Union Jack that fell away to reveal Triumph's new model to the audience at the Royal Garden Hotel in Kensington. Never has any factory managed such a successful development in such constrained circumstances. The 120mph 750cc TS8-1 had arrived and the workers had built their own 'superbike' worthy of the title. Incredibly, the Japanese police ordered several for trials with their own force. Finally Rosamund, Robinson and the greatly reduced workforce had cleared their bank loan. They were out of debt at last!

I threw my leg over the bike and rode to the centre of Meriden village. It was quiet and only enjoyed the services of a baker and hairdresser, both of which were closed. The buildings were 1930's style and set back behind long lawns. I figured that Meriden must have a lot of people who qualified for their free bus pass and it certainly felt as far removed from the source of a legend as you could get.

Over the road an old boy in a deerstalker strolled by. The village gamekeeper? Did he once see Mr Turner roar by every morning? Does he remember Steve McQueen stopping for a bacon butty before dropping in to the factory? Now for some living history I thought.

"Excuse me, can you tell me where the Triumph factory used to be?"
"Pardon?"

Stone deaf and probably because of all the world speed record bikes that used to be revved up outside the hairdressers. I repeated the question.

"I've only lived here three months."

In the early eighties the recession started to bite deep. Even without debt the workers needed more business and much was available from Third World police forces that needed a rugged and reliable motorcycle. However many were military dictators and the Co-operative was a principled left leaning business. Or as America's *Cycle World* magazine put it 'redder than the bleeding Bolshoi ballet'.

The recession could not have come at a worse time with hard nosed monetarism the prevailing school of thought. Anything 'constructive' was becoming habitually dismissed as being part of the dated 'smoke stack' industries and instead everyone was encouraged to become an estate agent. Alas the estate agents, instructed to secure the sale of the Meriden factory pending a move to a smaller site, were less successful than the workers were at making motorcycles. The delay proved deadly, but as ever with Triumph the old vessel still fired a deadly salvo whilst slipping beneath the waves. The Texan dealer, Big D, had an incredible 155 mph victory in the Battle of the Twins at Daytona on their TS8-1. Then at long last a consultancy firm looked at the Co-operative and advised that an advance of £1m to enable the workers to retool would bring long-term viability within reach. However this was followed by a rebuke for a local authority employee for his 'over enthusiasm in helping Triumph that went beyond the detachment normally expected of senior local government officers.' It must have been the first and last time the words 'over enthusiasm' and 'local government' were used in the same sentence.

At around this time Steve McQueen's life was drawing to a close. It was a long time since he, Don Brown and Bud Ekins had raced in the desert. In his final days he returned to his Uncle Claude's Hog Farm way down in Slater, Missouri. Maybe he reflected on his life on the red carpet or maybe desert tracks taken at speed. Don Brown recalled to the author:-

I think Steve became very Hollywood after he did 'The Great Escape' (Bud did some of the stunt work on that film). When Steve was dying he tried to reach me by phone but I was on a new assignment and my secretary didn't know who he was so she failed to call me, so I missed him.

Steve died a week later having failed to say goodbye to his old friend who had sold him his first Triumph. Never again would he fly to Meriden to see the bikes he loved being assembled by hand. Neither would he cause office girls to comment on how short he was in real life, or give a pair of his gloves to one of the workers. Years later there would be an indecent scrabble by manufacturers of motorcycles, clothing, watches and sunglasses to find some association between the 'King Of Cool' and their products. When his real gloves were found in a Coventry garage by the wife of the factory worker to whom they had been given, she threw them away thinking they were just any old pair of gloves.

Meanwhile the lack of a buyer for the Meriden site and the absence of an alternative smaller site cost critical time that the world-weary workforce did not have. The cash had run out and the odyssey of one of the most unequal struggles in British commercial history was drawing to a close. One of the members of the Workers' Co-operative would later recall that

We said we'd celebrate when we'd solved this problem or that problem. We never really did celebrate.

I followed the road out of the village. On my right ran a hedge that marked the border of the Triumph factory. Behind it lay a housing estate of 'executive' homes: Bonneville Close, Daytona Drive and there, under the dappled shade of a beech tree, was a stone memorial. In pewter was the casting of a man at speed on a Triumph under which were the words:-

> *THIS WAS THE SITE OF*
> *THE TRIUMPH MOTORCYCLE*
> *FACTORY MERIDEN*
> *1942 - 1983*

I rode by and out of the village to where the road feels as if it leads to nowhere, but it has simply been bypassed. The road that time forgot leads to the last remaining part of the Triumph factory. I eased up by the iron fence. It was rusted and the weeds grew up around this once proud factory. An old flagpole without a Union Jack remained at the corner of the building and behind the frosted windows was the incomprehensible shape of goods in storage. Despite there being half a dozen cars parked at the front there was no sign of any activity. In these very buildings they had prepared the bikes that conquered the world. I idly leant against the fence which had not seen a paint brush since at least 1983.

In the autumn of that same year, Mr Turner's glamorous daughter Charmian had visited the complete but silent factory for the last time. The Triumph logo was still above the main entrance but the flags were gone. Her father had commenced the Gaffers' Gallop from the same spot at which she was photographed for their private family album. The following day another film crew made its final visit to Meriden as people gathered at the gates in silence. They were knocking *our* factory down, or so it felt.

I rode back to the site of the demolition, now unrecognisable as a modern housing estate. An old lady in man-made fibres planted posies in her front garden as the wind tugged at her silver hair. She did not look up. The locals are used to the spectacle of sentimental motorcyclists photographing their street sign.

Throughout the day of the demolition there had been a succession of cars and motorcycles passing very slowly. At around mid-day a car turned the corner into Meriden's Main Street for the very last time. Inside was Ivor Jennings, the export manager who had suffered perpetual title changes at the hands of the consultants in the sixties. In his passenger seat was the very proper Nan Plant, Mr Turner's secretary for nearly four decades. Nan was a lady who had probably never sworn in her life. They both gazed from the car as the factory was being reduced to rubble and Nan uttered a very minor profanity. From her it summed up the moment as a crane swung an iron ball into Mr Turner's old office. After several stubborn attempts, it was no more.

THIS WAS THE SITE OF
THE TRIUMPH MOTORCYCLE
FACTORY MERIDEN
1942 - 1983
SCULPTRESS FRANCES FIRTH

SATURDAY NIGHT AND SUNDAY MORNING

Little troubled Mr Turner on Wednesday the 7th October, 1953. It had so far been a mild autumn and the Terriers moved swiftly through the traffic returning over 100 mpg. All was well. Back at the factory, a workforce used to his absences happily went about their business. The former apprentice turned author, Hughie Hancox recalled life under Mr Turner:-

> I've always likened him to the captain of a big ship. He held awesome power...he was somewhat of a bully...people couldn't easily sway him from his beliefs. I think the factory ran a lot better under the auspices of Mr Turner than it did later on.

This approach appears to have been effective. Mr Turner's 'little factory in England' was a happy place. Hughie recalls his first visit:-

> Row upon row of gleaming machines ...I had never seen so many bikes...but it was the smell, rubber, paint and petrol - as well as the sights and sounds which was simply marvellous.

And perhaps there was little market for films about content people. The illusion left from the era is that the factory was a dreary place that echoed to parochial accents. The luvvies could have made a film about the camaraderie of a motorcycle factory but instead they descended on the Raleigh cycle factory in Nottingham, to record for posterity the antics of a disaffected young rake played by Albert Finney. *Saturday Night And Sunday Morning* was another dose of that gritty 'realism', liberally punctuated with beer, sordid affairs and disillusionment. Despite this cocktail it was better than most films of the era and was repeated for decades and inadvertently helped to compound industry's 'smoke stack' image. Young Albert would spend his day at a lathe surrounded by old ladies in sexless marriages, leaving him to get his fun wherever he could in another of those places where the ghostly whistle of the last train signalled an early end to a night on the town.

The pub on the corner and the bus route was the limit of their world. Had they made it to the pictures it would have been for escapism and to bask in the rays of sunlight that American films cut through the mist and chimneys. But Albert's trouble was that he thought for himself. He was out to smash the glass ceiling and, like many people all over the country he wanted to know what was around the next corner. In many ways, Albert was a Triumph rider in waiting: a bad boy. One of the emerging ill-disciplined of the post National Service world that the Colonels of the Old Bell in Malmesbury 'would not like to lead into the jungle'. And his life was dull, his job was dull and he had little connection with the end product that bore his fingerprints. But the film's portrayal of limited aspirations and opportunities was chillingly accurate, although few in his position wanted to go to the movies to be reminded of their wretched plight.

Even with a truck load of sentiment it is hard to imagine that life in any Midlands factory in the 1950s differed greatly. However the workers at Meriden did care about their finished product and it showed. And even with his mercurial ways, Mr Turner could not berate young men from the factory floor who were tuning motorcycles at 10 pm even if the din had raised him from his office. Had the luvvies gone to Meriden rather than Nottingham they would probably have at least made their film in colour.

Hughie Hancox recounts the excitement of everyday in his book *Tales Of Triumph Motorcycles And The Meriden Factory*. For Hughie, Meriden was ultimately a human institution and the humanity shines through as he recalls:-

We were told to take the works van and go to ...rescue a family which had
broken down on a Triumph motorbike and sidecar".

It turned out to be a family taking their annual holiday with two small
children. They had resigned themselves to that holiday being ruined, but
without letting on, Triumph had other ideas. The family were taken to the
canteen for a drink while Hughie and a colleague simply rebuilt the bike,
Hughie continues:-

Although the bike was strictly out of warranty, I think the bill was waived
because of the circumstance prevailing and he'd only got enough money for his
holiday on him and we didn't want to spoil that.

They left amidst waves and good wishes having lost but a few hours. This
was the era before access to a factory was by means of retina recognition.
It was the human contact between the Meriden family and the public which
could only occur before the Brigadier arrived, that made it a place which
two small children never forgot.

For Hughie all this was coming to a brief end because, unlike the young
rake at the Raleigh factory, Hughie was packing his doss bag for two years
National Service. There was however a problem. The 'road to nowhere' that
I had discovered when I visited the old factory was part of a run on which
riders used to launch themselves up Meriden Hill. To this day there is an
old lamppost up there that bears the scars of a motorcycle accident where
Hughie had smashed his own Speed Twin in 1950.

Back then Hughie endured endless mickey taking; "if you fall off when
you work in a motorcycle factory I guess you must expect something like
this" he adds courageously. With his motorbike in bits and his mates pulling
his leg, he braced himself for his last day at work and did as he was told;
"well young man it's your last day, get on with something". That day wore
on with Hughie expecting his bike, presumably a collection of bent bits, to
be handed to him in assorted tea chests where it would have to remain until
his National Service was over. Or so he thought.

At last I saw JRW 405, but it wasn't my bike, as there was no number plate
on it. I couldn't believe it she was brand new: not only had the frame been
changed, there were new forks, petrol tank, mudguards, new sprung wheel...
Just then old Ted from the paint shop appeared with my front and rear number
plates..." look on it as a going away present". I was overwhelmed and escaped
to the toilets and cried.

Mr Turner was probably aware that on any of his numerous absences from the factory he was leaving behind a very human institution that was fundamentally a happy place. Perhaps that was not quite so rare during his tenure as it subsequently became.

Back on the Gaffers' Gallop in 1953, Mr Turner headed north through the Midlands and up to the Great North Road. The artery between the two capitals allows travellers to witness the change of topography as he passes through the lowlands, over meandering estuaries and rolling hills before the road ultimately reaches for the heavens north of the border. It links the provinces of simple parents to the streets of sin bejewelled wonder in London.

Mr Turner made his way to Bawtry and promptly left. It is merely a road sign that passes in a blur at which one never stops, unless you wish to avail yourself of the use of a transport café.

The truckers watched the traffic pass by as most people in Bawtry did and indeed do to this day. The increasingly out of breath Sunbeam-Talbot pulled up in the pot holed lorry park by the café as Frank Griffiths went in search of a bacon butty. In the glove box of the car were comprehensive sets of ESSO road maps, courtesy of that sponsor. Maps were for navigation and going on a journey was an adventure. The covers of the maps reflected the regions' distinctive features, Kent oast houses, East Anglian windmills, Yorkshire Dales and Scottish heather. The road had not diluted the nation but the nation was on the move. Petrol rationing had just finished and movement was becoming more widespread to a previously static class: those featured in *Saturday Night And Sunday Morning*. Their ancestors' movement had previously been resisted by the victor of Waterloo, The Duke of Wellington who opposed the railways because it 'encouraged the working classes to move around'. By the thirties, HV Morton wrote in his best selling *In Search Of England*:-

> *I have seen charabanc parties from the large manufacturing towns, providing a mournful text for an essay on progress, playing coronets on village greens and behaving with a barbaric lack of manners which might have been outrageous had it not been so unconscious, and therefore only pathetic.*

But after years of watching Spencer Tracy at the movies as he drove his Chevvy through the night over many a state boundary, the motorcar became firmly implanted as the new liberator.

Frank drove Mr Turner's car, which was the same model as immortalised by Cary Grant and Grace Kelly in *To Catch A Thief*. However Grace had the convertible to allow the warm breeze of the Riviera to catch her blond locks. Mr Turner had the fixed head coupe to protect him from the Coventry fog and its interior was still like a Pall Mall club. However the truckers would shortly be accompanied on the road by cars that owed more to Spencer Tracy and Marylyn Monroe than Noel Coward and the Queen Mother, for British manufacturers had started to produce cars to reflect a classless age. Their products sported fins and chrome with the more tasteless looking like mobile jukeboxes with interiors that had more in common with an American diner than a gentleman's club.

Frank tucked into his bacon butty and witnessed the dropping off of bus passengers. The café represented the end of the road for one bus company and the start for another, being one step closer to London. Each night would witness the heartache of runaway daughters and wayward sons as well as those who could not get served elsewhere; motorcyclists.

Frothy Italian coffee was served after the sun went down as the Ford Prefects and assorted Austins departed for suburban wives far more dependable than runaway girls. By midnight the café's fluorescent lights would be reflected in the chrome 'mouth organ' tank badge on Triumph petrol tanks. This huge 'tasteless' emblem was the product of the flowing pencil of Mr Turner's designer of four decades, Jack Wickes. It had the sweeping lines of the Triumph logo set against a bed of criss-crossed chrome. In contrast, motorcycles like Vincents and Velocettes frequently had their rider's coat of arms discreetly painted about the tank. But if your family did not have a coat of arms then you belonged to the new age of mass production. That age brought 100mph to the very people the Duke of Wellington wanted to contain. Mr Turner had no idea what he was doing and had Frank Griffiths hung around in the café he would have seen the trade in records brought in by merchant sailors back from America. Something called Rock 'n' Roll was on its way and would bring a primordial jungle beat that made the blood course through young motorcyclists' veins and be held responsible for a surge in delinquency. Consequently transport cafés enjoyed a seedy reputation and their lights attracted the wayward like moths to a light. Sherborne educated social critic Richard Hoggart got all frothy on the subject:-

> There is one in almost every Northern town…which has become the regular rendezvous of some young men. Girls go to some, but most customers are boys aged between fifteen and twenty, with drape suits picture ties and an American slouch.

Best press one's brogues on the accelerator and hope not to be embarrassed by a young hood who makes his living in some oil soaked railway siding. Ain't misbehavin'? They soon will be!

Mr Turner was making good time as he passed the old aerodromes that had seen so much activity during the war, now somewhat quieter. He made his way to the town the locals call Bonny Donny and he accurately deduced that Doncaster was anything but Bonny and pressed on. He was heading for the wide open skies of the North Country and he would not be disappointed.

THOSE TEXANS WILL BE BACK

I pulled up outside the National Motorcycle Museum on the very spot where Richard and Mopsa English had been photographed having circumnavigated the globe on a Triumph donated by the Workers' Co-op. They had departed with a handshake from the leader of the Co-operative and returned to a handshake from the founder of a museum.

Today it was drizzling and I had an audience with an indifferent crowd of reps on a fag break all neatly labelled with identity tags. I strolled past life size photographs of racing legends and was met by the magnificent odour of polish and oil. There at the turnstile was a little man waving his arms about, "Now-buddy towld mee 'ee was coomeen"

This I deduced was my host Dave and went over to give him a good firm handshake in the time honoured tradition that meant so much to Mr Turner's generation. Dave turned out to be a genial host who led me through this vast citadel of motorcycling where we prepared for a photoshoot surrounded by literally tons of Mr Turner's Triumphs.

We passed by one of the museum's 150cc Terriers and one look at that saddle made my eyes water. To think that Mr Turner had sat on that for over a thousand miles, or at least those miles when he was not asleep in the back of the Sunbeam-Talbot.

At the photo shoot there was Dave and I meeting, Dave and I talking, Dave and I in contemplation. We tried to make it all look candid with Dave in one shot determinedly stabbing his finger at the speedometer as if a goblin had appeared behind the glass.

"Sometimes I don't like to say too much in case I say something really styoopeed", said Dave as he looked up at me from under his comb over. Dave was an obliging host which more than made up for his lack of television presence.

"You've got the best job on earth Dave", I added unable to help but feel reflective amongst all this beautiful machinery. And then I saw something.

"Dave is that what I think it is?"

Whatever his reply was I did not hear, for there in front of me was a real legend in all its svelte missile like glory. Probably the most famous motorcycle in the world; Stormy Mangham's Streamliner, aka the very first Triumph Bonneville.

My imagination took me back to this bike's era: the fifties. Consequently it no longer felt like a rainy day in June just off junction 6 of the M42. It was a Saturday night in 1953 at Pete Dalio's Triumph workshop, Fort Worth, Texas. An exclusive bunch of enthusiasts were playing poker into the small hours surrounded by crates of Triumphs and racing trophies. Dalio's tuner, Jack Wilson had served his country in the war as had former aviator Captain JH 'Stormy' Mangham. It was the wrong time and the wrong place to suggest that the land speed record being in the hands of Willi Hertz and the German NSU team was evidence that they were the 'master race'. There was no rational debate followed by a group hug for the nutter in their midst. In Texas it's deeds that count, not words and Stormy said nothing but his message was loud and clear.

In some ways Stormy was to motorcycling what that smooth talkin' Texan, Carol Shelby was to the AC Cobra sports car: a guy who did it his way. But it was 'planes that brought him his nickname and twisters and typhoons did not keep Stormy on the ground. Jack Wilson recalled:-

In the early days flying those mail planes could be a dangerous business. They had to keep up to schedule and if big storms were raging, the pilots got extra pay. But even so quite a few preferred not to risk it. But Stormy always volunteered so when the boss came into the crew room asking for volunteers the rest of the guys would say "Stormy will take it" and with that the name stuck. In fact I never did know his first name.

Stormy assembled a team of amateurs and set out to take the world speed record from a huge German engineering concern with almost limitless backing. He relied on famous Texan initiative applied late at night in the garages of determined private individuals. It would become one of the greatest stories seldom told outside the motorcycling world.

By contrast the NSU team was thirty strong, had factory facilities, access to Stuttgart University's wind tunnel and were mates with the President of the Federation Internationale De Motocyclisme. However Stormy had good mates, a garage full of spanners and a lesson to teach someone. None of this made up for the shortage of a wind tunnel, so Stormy attached balsa wood models to the outside of his cockpit, set out across the dark wild expanses and measured the resistance each shape offered. Thus Stormy's Streamliner was born of glassfibre wrapped around a Triumph engine, based on a bit of wood.

Willi Hertz first set a record of 180.39 mph on a German Autobahn in 1951. New Zealander Russel Wright took this from him on a Vincent at 184.94 mph. The Germans got it back as an advert for their great engineering empire built on all the surplus metal from the left-over tanks and stuff. Unfortunately Adolf had not built an Autobahn long enough for the increasing speeds and they had to make their way to the Holy Grail of land speed records, the Bonneville Salt Flats in Utah.

Around the same time Stormy set off on his own to try out his creation.

It's my design and I want to see if it works. I don't want to make a fool of anybody but me.

First time out on a standard engine with twin carburettors he topped 150 mph. Never underestimate what a bloke can get up to in a garage! When Stormy came back he enlisted local legend Jack Wilson, to work on the engine. Fifty years later top American magazine, *Cycle World* would open an obituary to Jack Wilson with the words:-

A cruel, unforgiving mistress, the Bonneville Salt Flats. She breaks more hearts than she allows land speed records to be taken. Bonneville always liked Jack Wilson though.

During the winter of 1955 Jack reworked the standard engine so that when it next saw the light of day it ran on a nitrous methanol mix and turned out twice as much brake horse power as the Triumph factory had ever managed to squeeze out of one of their own.

On the first run, a wiry Texan, Johnny Allen who, like Jack Wilson was part native American, 'went down the salt' at 191 mph when the tyres gave way. The record was not recognised by the Federation but in Texas they did not recognise the Federation either and it's a big state.

Contradictory accounts exist as to whether the anti-racing Mr Turner knew, encouraged or even assisted with the record attempt. One thing is certain, the credit belongs to a bunch of 'good ole boys' from Fort Worth;

without them Triumph would have been deprived of their most famous model.

Triumph importers Jo Mo heard of Stormy's efforts and knew the commercial impact success would have. Their man, Wilbur Cedar was on the phone to England and enlisted Neale Shilton's help and he in turn was instrumental in getting special tyres made that would hold together at over 200 mph on a salt bed.

Even if the Federation did not recognise Johnny's record, everyone else did, particularly the Germans and on the 2nd of August 1956 they found conditions 'on the salt' were good. Willi Hertz would raise the outright record to 210.86 mph, beating everyone fair and square and they consequently had every right to slap their lederhosen. The NSU publicity machine was duly cranked up and the thirty strong team, including the President of the Federation, packed their bags and drove down the strip one last time before leaving Bonneville. They were not sorry. There is not a lot to do if you are not breaking speed records and the International Raceway has only one town nearby: Wendover. The only reason Wendover is there at all is because it is a station stop for the Union Pacific Railroad. The town still runs to Mountain Time rather than Pacific Time and the residents wish they were in Nevada, just footsteps away so they could legally gamble. However, at least they have their own airstrip but not because people want to go there, but precisely because they do not and it is out of sight. Here the USAF trained the aircrew of the Enola Gay. If the government wants to get up to anything naughty they could not find a better place than the remote Tooele County that houses Wendover and a population that takes part in TV phone-ins about UFO sightings.

When the raceway was just a geographical phenomena with only motorhomes and tents once a year, the speed freaks had to find an area to work at night. If they were lucky they would be allowed to use the all night Texaco service station. Here the victorious German team loaded up as the salt bitten old garage hand served them at the pumps. He found them arrogant as he took their money and cast his mind back to his agreeable acquaintanceship with Stormy's band of merry amateurs. Leaning into the lead vehicle, he grabbed the driver by the collar and pulled him closer to aid his hearing, adding 'those Texans will be back'. And 33 days later, they were back.

However it was a David and Goliath battle and in his book *A Million Miles Ago*, Neale Shilton comments:-

The Germans must have smiled benevolently at the garage built streamliner
as they went away to proclaim the world's fastest machine at the Cologne
exhibition.

The Texans watched the dawn break over Bonneville on the 6th of
September, 1956. A black stripe was painted onto the salt for the rider
to follow when the world takes on its incomprehensible dimension at
over 200 mph. Stormy's Streamliner was placed on the stripe pointing
to the distant hills that were already shimmering in the gathering heat
haze. The previous evenings moisture had evaporated off the salt and the
time keeping crew signalled that they were ready. Rescue vehicles were
positioned at intervals down the strip as the early morning silence was
finally broken by the Triumph bursting into life. Stormy and Jack held up
the machine as the engine growled it's warm up note whilst Johnny Allen
was at the controls, the loneliest man in the world. The seconds ticked by
until the Streamliner was finally pushed away, rapidly disappearing into
the distance. It was the only sound to be heard on the salt flats as the near
standard, solitary 650cc engine gathered speed. After a mile following the
black stripe and focussing on the distant mountains, the bike was up to
speed. The electronic starting beam was broken by a blur inside which was
an unnaturally cool Johnny Allen.

Stormy and Jack never spoke as the speed of the first run was confirmed.
Their months of effort were put to the test in such a short space of time yet
it did not feel like that when waiting for it to pass. Thirty three days earlier
on this very spot the mighty NSU team had shared the burden between
themselves, the President of FIM and the world's press. Now two small
specks from the Lone Star state were doing it their way.

The signal came back from the timekeeper; 213 mph. It all depended on
the return run to calculate the average. What drove these two silhouettes in
the salt would be recalled by Jack Wilson years later:-

What really bugged us though, was a US Army colonel of German extraction.
He was named Kohne and he had come around here later bragging about the
Germans and their record.

The return run was about to turn this moment to a point in history as
the bike was turned and Johnny wound back the throttle once more. The
Streamliner's note was at a constant 7,500 rpm as it broke the beam again
and emerged through the heat haze. It was roaring flat out as the atmosphere
seared over its nose cone, guided by Johnny's steady hand. He closed down

the throttle once the run was complete and silence quickly returned to the salt flats as the waiting began.

The time keepers could not believe it: a hand built machine out of a Texas shed had travelled faster than any motorcycle on earth: the average speed was 214.17 mph. How long can Hollywood overlook Stormy, Jack and Johnny and, for the record, the rest of the team: Bus Schaller, Skip Fordyce, Wilbur Ceder, Lyle Hysert, Tom Ryan, Jess Thomas and Dick Ragan?

The Federation duly telegraphed their congratulations, NSU cancelled its Cologne exhibition celebrations and then the President, who had hung out with the Germans, tried to cancel recognition of the Texan's record. What happened next frankly stunk like a skunk. The Federation again refused to recognise the record, Mr Turner found out, went 'ape shit' as only he could and 'hauled his ass off to court'. A day's headline for breaking the land speed record turned into eight months of publicity for a legal dispute, by which time the Triumph brand was synonymous with world records anyway.

Back at Mr Turner's 'little factory in England' the very first production Triumph Bonneville had yet to take shape. Mr Turner had opposed increasing his 500cc twin to 650, had opposed racing, and indeed twin carburettors. The Bonneville, Triumph's most famous motorcycle would have to be treated carefully if it was to make the fraught journey from idea to metal. Neale Shilton takes up the story:-

> I approached the top man very diplomatically and I began by saying that no doubt he had already thought of the proposal I wished to make. I recommended a more sporting appearance of a twin carburettor motor. The machine would be called the Bonneville with two colour finish of Utah sky blue and salt flats white. There was a long pause interrupted only by the tapping of the Turner pencil, which was usually an ominous sign.

Gently Neale prized approval out of Mr Turner and in the darkened caverns of the Meriden factory, an engine the apprentices called 'the monster' went through its promising tests. In early 1959 the bike was put together and presented by Mr Turner himself to the motorcycle press whereupon it refused to start. Neale finally managed to get it to start but only on one cylinder that naturally sounded dog rough. This enraged Mr Turner, caused the press to snigger and Neale to fear for his job. Mr Turner was ready to call off production of this legend in waiting when Neale presented him with a bent valve and the news that one of the press had ridden it like a racer, missed a gear change and sent the revs soaring. Mr Turner sat there like Caesar before the Bonneville finally got his nod but by then it was too late to put it in that year's publicity brochure. Late in 1959 the first Triumph Bonneville rolled off the production line and a legend was born. The Bonnie put the most expensive sports cars to shame, went through incarnations where it was slimmed down, chromed up and became the embodiment of the lean skeletal no frills machine. From every angle it looked right, sounded like thunder and its raffish image appealed to the very people the Honda 'nicer people' publicity machine wanted to avoid. In time it acquired the dubious distinction of being statistically more likely to be stolen or involved in an accident than any other motorcycle on the road.

But legends are invariably the creation of accident and the Bonnie stayed the way it was born because of under investment. Financial misjudgements lead to the preservation of an antique design that evolved from 'old hat' to renaissance as the decades rolled by. The Bonnie was born before the disposable lifestyle and survived it. American magazine *Cycle World* understood:-

> *It's always interesting to test a new Triumph but not because they differ from year to year. It's because they incorporate subtle changes which brings them a little closer to the ideal American riders expect from their machines*

For those bikers who wanted something 'real', there was simply no contest. But in January 1983 the last Bonnie left Meriden and in June 1985 the first rolled off a new production line in Devon, just like I always knew that somehow, somewhere they would. The launch of a 'new' motorcycle is usually a plush affair at a swanky London hotel, brimming with nobs in suits quaffing complimentary champagne. But this was different and new owner Les Harris, speaking from the arches by London's Ace Café on the North Circular, chose to explain the impact of the Bonnie on his misspent youth:-

> *...I got chased once by two Speed Twins and two police cars and I didn't feel like stopping so I left them, I went straight through Roundwood Park, straight through a football team and I was touching 100 mph up through the side streets of Willesden. Unfortunately I got banned for two years for that.*

Company directors just wanna have fun!

The world was changing and bureaucrats, whose only personal contribution to saving the planet is to fly economy when shopping for high efficiency light bulbs, were making 'environmental' laws. They decided that the golden rumble was too loud and 1988 saw the last Turner designed Triumph roll off the production line. And that should have been the end of the line for Mr Turner's motorcycle, but it's not called a legend for nothing.

A mysterious new purpose built motorcycle factory appeared in Leicestershire. The bikes that emerged had little to do with the thundering Triumphs of old except the name. Indeed the engineering owed much to the superb Japanese standards and quite deliberately nothing to the white knuckle ride and old world charm of what original Triumph owners called the 'real thing'. Triumph were out to prove that they could beat the Japanese at their own game and then add some quality to carve out their very own niche.

Back in Texas, the 'good ole boys' were up to their old tricks with Triumph's new multi cylindered engines. Their next generation of speed record bikes sported a logo that read 'Made In England Made Greater In Texas'.

Jack Wilson was Mr Bonneville and no other machine went to the hearts of so many riders worldwide. Stormy and Jack made a legend and between 1955 and 1990 Jack built over 65 record breaking Triumphs. The American importers ran an advert in the mid '70s which read 'Triumph have been setting land speed records here longer than most motorcycles have been in production' and of course the setting was Bonneville Salt Flats. Of the thirty six speed records that Triumph then held, twenty four of them had come out of Jack Wilson's workshop and that is why there is a little corner of Meriden that is forever Texas.

Back at the new Triumph factory they had cut a segment of the market for themselves and were establishing a following of their own that stood entirely independent of any association with Mr Turner's Triumphs. It was now safe to look again at their most famous model, the Bonnie. But on Sunday the 7th of May, 2000 Jack Wilson breathed his last. More important than the legend he and Stormy created, he left behind a wife of forty-nine years, four children, ten grandchildren and six great grandchildren. Across the Triumph world people spoke of their friend first and foremost, even if earning Jack's friendship was not always easy, the following lines from his eulogy indicate that it was worth the effort:-

> It always annoyed Jack that he and Johnny received so much credit and so little mention was made of Stormy Mangham. Jack said many a time, "It was Stormy that conceived and built that Streamliner. Without Stormy it would never have happened".

And without Stormy a thoroughly modern big twin cylinder, Turner styled Triumph Bonneville would not have rolled off the new production line half a century later. When parked next to an original Bonnie it takes a second glance to find a distinction. And as if by way of a rowdy reminder not to forget who really made the legend, the Royal Signals White Helmets Motorcycle Display Team needed their own Turner Triumphs replacing. The last production run was built by the Army from spares and resulted in thirty full metal motorcycles bursting into an increasingly sanitised age. It was sixty four years since Mr Turner built his first 500cc Speed Twin from which it had evolved.

The new Bonnie went straight to the top of the sales charts and to the commercially astute Triumph that was all that mattered.

In front of Stormy's Streamliner at the National Motorcycle Museum is one of the first Triumph Bonnevilles from 1959. Its paint finish is eggshell blue for the Utah sky and tangerine for the burning desert.

Dave brought me to with "It all got burned down you know". He went on to tell me that in 2003 70% of the museum was destroyed and that included Stormy's Streamliner. Immediately, Texan friends of Stormy and Jack set up a 'Save Our Streamliner' campaign. With project manager Dennis Thacket at the helm of a 'motley crew' (his words not mine) they set out to rebuild the Streamliner. Incredibly the original moulds were found at the back of a workshop where they had been gathering dust since 1956.

The Museum's owner and my sponsor, the late Roy Richards, would spend £20 million over 15 months to restore the museum. He commented to Dennis Thacket:-

> Our motto is 'Where Legends Live On', and we will honour that statement by rebuilding the museum.

To which Dennis replied "and we will do the same to the Streamliner". And that's exactly what they did. On the 6th of September, 2004 exactly forty-eight years to the day from the original record being taken, Stormy's Streamliner made one last visit to the Bonneville Salt Flats before flying home to a newly restored Museum.

The year 2009 represented the 50th anniversary of the first production Bonnie. The new Triumph Company produced 650 limited edition models to commemorate the occasion. The colour scheme was eggshell blue for the Utah sky and tangerine for the burning desert.

It may have been raining as I strode out of the museum but to me it felt very much like the Texan sun was on my back.

JUST PASSIN' THRU

In 1953 school children sat down at their desks to read the following description of the county in which Mr Turner found himself:-

> *Every Yorkshire boy will tell you that Yorkshire has an acre for every letter in the Bible and some left over, and the traveller who sets out to explore it is not surprised, for its vast spaces seem to have no end.*

Yorkshire people have always been proud of their county and they have much to be proud of. The picture of England may be one of cream teas in Surrey gardens but up here they 'keep it real'.

To the west and adjacent to the Great North Road, runs the London to Edinburgh railway line which was graced by the flowing lines of the Mallard train as it expelled steam into the autumn air, blah blah blah. You have heard it all before and it's too romantic to be entirely true, which is a pity. A more accurate image to reflect these 'ye olde' times gone by would be the perfect delta winged symmetry of Britain's V–bombers in those quieter world war two aerodromes to the east of the road. The reason they were quieter was that fewer planes could deliver more devastating bombs as was their wont. Ladies may still have made jam at home and received the milk from horse drawn vehicles, but now we could melt the planet and were gearing up to do so. Still, you would sell more tins of biscuits at a garden fete if they had a Neolithic steam train chuffing towards Edinburgh pictured on the tin lid, rather than a solitary Vulcan screaming over the Urals en route to Leningrad.

Adjacent to all this radioactive sabre rattling, Yorkshire folk still lived up to their reputation for appreciating a bargain. Nowhere on earth would the words '100 mpg' get sombre flat-capped souls to rise from the fireside to show their appreciation. Economy - the word was invented in Yorkshire. Economy in all things it appears, even those that are free, like place names. Mr Turner's route passed through Hooton Pagnall, Slade Hooton, Hooton Levitt, Hooton Roberts, Hooton Luxury, Hooton You Were Lucky and Hooton Tell 'Em Today And They Don't Believe You. Long after rationing had ended Yorkshire folk continued with the cult of thrift. They throw nowt away and they like nowt swanky and anyone who does gets met with the greeting 'ayup who the bloody 'ell do you think you are?' If you like to show off, do it in any other county but Yorkshire for you are held in higher esteem for riding a 100mpg Terrier than driving a Rolls Royce. In fact the favourite competition is the reverse of that played out in other counties: the desire to prove yourself the poorer. Uncomfortable souls in the South East of England may have stretched themselves to keep up with the neighbours but in Yorkshire it is the other way round.

Moving through what the locals modestly call 'God's Country', Mr Turner left behind the mining and railroad communities of South Yorkshire and entered the rural money belt. Terraced houses and slag heaps quickly gave way to a greener more open countryside where you had the road to yourself. Eventually the historic Minster at York rose out of the flatlands and Mr Turner pressed on with the road slowly rising as the wind turned fresher as it tugged at the grass verge. If in any doubt why they call this God's Country, Mr Turner only had to glance both east and west as he took the high road towards Boroughbridge. Magnificent farmland swept across the plain before rising to the North York Moors to the east. The west-facing slope sports the giant chalk image of the White Horse of Kilburn that is visible from miles away. To the west beyond the ranks of hedgerows, woodland and regimented ploughed fields rose the dark and forbidding Pennines and in the misty distance the Scottish border. God's country, ain't no mistakin'.

The fingerpost road signs all pointed to Boroughbridge with its sharp right then left-hand bend into the market square. Somewhere in the Turner family album I expect there lies a photograph of the three Terriers and Mr Turner, Fearon and Masters alongside the well in the market square. Here they stopped for lunch, in a town far better acquainted with green wellies and Land Rovers than any of their rather grander destinations. The locals served real ale and ploughman's in this tiny old town as the Gaffers became acclimatised to the slightly fresher feel as the rays of sunlight swept across the square before being chased away by dark scudding clouds.

Outside people got on with their business. Those from out of town parked up, picked up their provisions and repaired to outlying farms. In the newsagents, local motorcyclists dropped in and had a choice between two weekly publications; the 'green un' and the 'blue un' as *MotorCycling* and *The Motor Cycle* were respectively known on account of the colour of their covers. In the pages of the latter, Canon Basil Henry Davies, known to readers as Ixion, would dispense his wise counsel, not always in keeping with theological doctrine. Indeed when once asked if there were motorcycles in heaven he mischievously answered, 'Of course, or there would be no point in going'. However, it is his observation of *Inns Large And Small* that is worth consideration for the writer who endeavoured to follow years later with a tent:-

Sheer luxury quickly becomes incredibly boring and monotonous.

Consequently he ended up selecting 'unknown roadside inns' when on the road himself with dramatic consequences:-

Out of a world of insincerity and monotony and money grabbing we should step into a world of variety and reality.

Outside, the autumn breeze tumbled off the lip of the moors, swept across the vale and bent the copse behind the market square. Rooks lifted gently into the sky as they looked down on three Triumphs parked around the well. The road was calling once again.

WOW, KICK ARSE!

"What's this guy doing in the fast lane?" I muttered to myself.

"About 130mph" shouted the gremlin on my shoulder. Don't try this at home folks.

Dave's directions turned out to be excellent and I wished he had been around when I was searching for the Imperial Hotel in Exeter. Consequently I made it to the new Triumph factory from the National Motorcycle Museum in the available thirty minutes. Ho hum, just joshing officer.

I passed through security on a fairly anonymous Hinckley industrial estate and had my breath taken away. There before me was something akin to a James Bond film set in which the man with the white cat plans to take over the world. I now faced the biggest building I had ever seen in my life. The new Triumph factory is the length of an airfield and the height of a tower block. The entrance is made from three storeys of black tinted glass inverted at an angle. Above this is another storey into which is set the famous Triumph logo and, to that extent only, it is just like old times. When I had my photograph taken, I had to get someone to walk backwards as far as Wales to get the whole building in. Mr Turner would have been impressed.

I passed through the entrance with a bristling chin and matted hair whilst trying to look cool. I have been in merchant banks that are less well appointed than this. Around thirty guests had gathered and were equally breathless at the citadel of modern motorcycling. Incredible that people should ask 'do they still make them today?'

I looked for Peter Clarke, the factory tour guide with whom I had briefly corresponded when making my plans for the Gaffers' Gallop. Coverage in *The Times* and eleven other publications, features on two foreign websites as well as my own and being a geezer in a suit with a penchant for leather (so to speak) made me a target client. Then I picked up their factory magazine and saw that they had pressed an interview with Viscount Linley in one copy and the Hollywood actor Hugh Laurie in the other and must have realised that they would not be able to cope with demand if Nigel C Winter was featured in a third.

I sat back and viewed the scene. I had leaned against the rusted railings at the old Triumph factory, touched the stone of a memorial and passed through a museum to over one hundred long gone manufacturers. Now I strode through some of Britain's most productive real estate, to which the publicity generated by my own Gaffers' Gallop had played its small but heroic part.

I shook Peter's hand as he looked over his assembled flock and awaited the arrival of a coach load from Doncaster. He advised me I might be lucky enough to meet a man called 'Bruno The Boss' and went on to mingle with the other guests. As the rain slat against those expensive windows, I suppose it was inevitable that only I would be daft enough to turn up on a motorbike and was starting to feel distinctly underdressed, particularly if I was going to meet Bruno.

I had spotted a couple of suntanned righteous bikers sporting tattoos and beards. It turned out that they were from New Zealand and I overheard one of them talking about the TT races, "I went to Bushy's bar to have my photograph taken, just to prove to the boys back home that I'd been to the Isle of Man", said the adventurous one to his mate who by contrast conveyed proof of his trip to Massachusetts by way of an Indian motorcycle T-shirt. They both had a couple of large ladies in tow whom I figured kept them warm whilst they rode around the world raising hell and collecting bugs in their teeth, (biker slang for cruising).

"Have you got the bike to go with the T-shirt?" I enquired,

"Hell I wish I had" came the response during which he nearly looked at me. These guys were clearly homesick and talk soon returned to the births deaths and marriages column in good old Auckland.

Peter was a busy man as he looked with grave concern at the skies and wondered about the well being of the coach party.

Triumph as a whole are busy and even though they produce more bikes now than at any at any time in their one hundred and some year history, they still keep a fairly low profile. You cannot blame them because the British media love nothing more than to see their own fail and Triumph are a very image conscious brand. When they do creep into the press it is usually in the financial pages as their success is becoming hard to ignore. Typical headlines read, 'Motorcycle Makers Move Up A Gear'. Turnover at around the £200 million mark, output up by 29% and operating profits up. It is all up, as is their street credibility courtesy of another generation of Hollywood stars. In the meantime that generation that is now sentimental about muddy pop festivals and cannabis, when they should be fixing a high fibre diet, can buy the same style Triumph T-shirt as worn by Bob Dylan on the cover of *Highway 61 Revisited*. You do not have to paint 'Triumph' across the back of your leather jacket any more as today's riders are more likely to work in the City than in some old railway siding and do not have time for personalised sartorial expression. And then to cap it all there is an array of watches, cuff links, tie clips and pens and anything else that bikers need when roaring down to the coast to have a dust up with scooter bound accountants from the Treasury.

Peter came away from the reception desk,

"OK folks, it looks like the coach from Doncaster can't get through the floods, so if you could take a factory pass and follow me", and with that the climbing began until we reached the presentation room where Peter dispensed tea and biscuits with the words "no expense spared". We filed into rows of seats and I found myself next to a silver haired yachtsman in moccasins with a plummy accent.

"What bike do you ride?" I enquired.

"I don't. My business partner had this booked but had to go abroad at the last minute so I am keeping his wife company". The lady next to him leaned forward and smiled. Yes she's got that 'somebody else's wife' look about her. It was the combination of my finely honed lawyer's instinct combined with the odour of claret that lead me to this conclusion.

"Good afternoon" said Peter to which no one except Captain Birdseye next to me confidently responded with "and good afternoon to you too". And with that we were off. The slide show began as Peter took us through Triumph's history, which conclusively showed that they had even beaten Harley Davidson to their centenary. Meanwhile Captain Birdseye's head started lolling before finally coming to rest on my shoulder where it slept soundly.

Triumph had in fact reached their centenary sometime earlier as the original company can be traced back to 1885. However I did not feel like raising this as I really wanted to avoid drawing attention to having a sailor's head resting on my shoulder.

Peter was in full flow when someone kicked the door open and announced "Ayup, us bastard river's bost its banks". Pete from Donny; a small man with big feet and dyed blond hair had arrived. Pete marshalled his coach load into their seats and slumped next to me, catching my eye whereon he nodded and greeted me with "arite our kid?". But that was not the end of it as there were now two people giving the talk both of whom happened to be called Peter. Peter went through the models and performance figures, "I can get a bloody site more than that", proffered Pete. The petrol consumption, "he's about right I reckon" and the rebirth of the Bonneville, " 'bout bloody time too". So there I was sat with Captain Birdseye asleep on my left shoulder and Pete on my right advising, " just teck silencers off n' coppers'll never catch yer. Well they didn't me but they daren't drive through Donny after dark anyway".

Peter continued "and we have the biggest research and development department of any motorcycle company in the world and that includes the big four", by which he means Honda, Kawasaki, Yamaha and Suzuki.

We were all handed intercom earpieces and then taken through the factory. It was surgically clean and hummed with activity. We watched rows of gloved craftsmen measuring and marking crankcases with studied intensity. Those parts that are not assembled by hand are done so by computer controlled machines. Making a motorcycle is as simple as this: the engine comes off the line and joins the chassis suspended in air. Exhaust and handlebars come next and slowly it starts to look like a motorcycle. Add the wheels, the brakes, all the fluids and it goes through yet another dollop of quality control. A total of three and a half hours from a pile of bolts to a motorcycle to fire up. Lawdy Mamma.

My own bike is standing in the rain with a broken rev counter. With all these tonnes of spares lying around, I am sure they would not feel the loss if they donated a new one. I thought I would put this to Peter but I was having trouble with my headset at which point Donny Pete handed me his, "Dunt worry cock, I've bin 'ere so many times I know what he's gonna say next". And with that we moved to the final packing section with bikes being loaded up for America, Japan, France and Australia. But it was not this that stopped me in my tracks. It was the small band of Co-op Veterans, plucked literally from Meriden's rubble and found a place in this hi-tech factory in which they could apply their ancient craft. The new Triumph Company deliberately sought them out and the coach painters that applied by hand the fabulous sculpted lines to Mr Turner's Triumphs did so to my very own 900cc Thunderbird. They are dwindling in number, advancing in years but at least they now have Christmas presents, nought per cent finance and peer pressure to shop at Ikea like the rest of us . And I am sure they are happier now than they were the year they held their heads high and walked through the Meriden factory gates for the children's Christmas party. But I wondered if amidst the chaos of a modern Christmas where grandchildren find greater interest in the wrapping than the content, if they ever cast their minds back to that very different era.

"Yer alright cock?" enquired Pete.

I cast my mind back to the eve of the demolition. One of those anonymous onlookers who drove passed was a time served apprentice. He stopped by the factory gates for one last photograph before boarding a 'plane taking him to a new life in Australia. He was through with Britain and with motorcycles. He now works for a Triumph dealership in Australia.

No sign of the Donny boys joining me drowning in sentiment as they whooped it up. One of their number, a young bloke with a ponytail sat on a mighty 2.2 litre Rocket Three, "I say Peter, can you sell this young man a motorbike?" asked Donny Pete placing his hand on Ponytail's shoulder like the patriarch I had no doubt he was. I subsequently fell into conversation with Ponytail and when he heard what I was doing he looked at me and exclaimed "Wow, kick arse!" Given that he was about half my age, I felt quite chuffed.

Sadly the time for my departure had come and the Donny boys filed through the doors and braced themselves for the long walk to security. Peter came out and told me that Bruno The Boss was unavailable so it was just he and me for the photographs at the factory's entrance. As I set the camera up I was a little concerned that my Dad's kind attempts to save me some money by fixing the rev counter would catch Peter's disapproving eye. Where once there had been a dial that counted thousands of revs there was now a seed marker from his green house. And the glass had been taken from an old welding mask that lay in a barn for years and had been adopted as a litter tray by the farm cats. Its unique odour had been reactivated by the wet weather and was not destined to do much to 'further enhance the brand'.

Photographs over and with Peter gone, I marvelled at all before me as well as my homemade rev counter. It was growing dark due to the heavy clouds and the lights were going out one by one behind me as I made my way to security. Through the gates and the Kiwi's were followed into their tired Mondeo by their large ladies who compressed the rear suspension. Bugs in my teeth indeed.

In the distance, Pete counted the last of the Donny boys onto the coach, placing his hand on Ponytail's shoulder once more before giving him the benefit of his wisdom, "Ya dunt want one of them bloody big motorbikes cock". But it was too late. Ponytail was on his mobile to his wife.

So who is behind all this? Not a 'celebrity tycoon' who makes a fast buck by selling kiddies mobile phones or expensively branded coffee for our casino economy. He is an unsentimental private individual, son of a Derbyshire miner and one time plasterer. Triumph's new owner, John Bloor, was seen as something of a mystery at the outset. This was probably because he liked his privacy, which one has to respect in an age when the positively talent-less trip over themselves to get on television. His lifetime of astute decisions lead to the creation of this state of the art monument to the actual making of things: we don't do much of that in Britain these days. It all felt a long way from the motorcycle industry of old when it was :-

Essentially unaltered for five decades and intended for rugged proletarians willing to brave the weather swaddled from helmeted top to booted toe.

Now no one would say of John (as Mr Bloor is known to his staff), what they said of Jack Sangster; that he was the 'wrong sort' because happily these are very different times.

Donny Pete's coach turned the corner as the passenger's all clapped in time and sang 'ere we go, 'ere we go, 'ere we go'. All except Ponytail who was by now pleading and promising to take his wife shopping for shoes every weekend until hell freezes over.

On my own once more and the only illumination was the intercom on security. I just could not resist it. I strolled over, pressed it and announced, "Hi guys, it's Ewan and Charlie", at which point the factory lit up like a Christmas tree.

I pulled out of Jacknalls Way Industrial Estate and into the evening rush hour. Slowly I made my way east catching an occasional glimpse of the Donny bus as the incumbents sung to their hearts content, up hill and down dale.

The weather improved as I made my way into the open countryside of middle England and its fields of swaying barley. Soon I happened upon the pork pie capital of the world, Melton Mowbray, but resisted the temptation and pressed on. In a week's time I would be amongst the ranks of the rush hour but for the time being I was happy to be apart from it.

Lanes and byways over I swung the Thunderbird onto the Great North Road. Normally full of traffic, but in this week of dire travel warnings; the wide straight road was incongruously quiet. Easing up at the bridge over the mighty Trent I surveyed the flood plain below. This is our Mississippi: a river and network of canals leading from the industrial heartland to the fertile lowlands out east. Today all the waterways have merged into one. The gravel pits in which shift workers normally fish at all times of night and day were indistinguishable. Canal barges were adrift as the sun set and cast a golden glow on the iron-span bridge in the middle of the flood. This is one waterway where the direction signs outnumber those on the road. They made little sense tonight.

I broke away from the scene and hit the road again. Bawtry passed in a blur and I entered Yorkshire. The very first house in the county is known as number one Yorkshire; the postman needs to know little else, it is that kind of county. Occasional convoys of traffic caught up with me but for the most part I was on my own. Diversions due to the floods lead me through the old mining villages of South Yorkshire. The locals soon found their lanes blocked with people who would usually scream passed on the motorway. Now they sat in their cars going nowhere as I filtered by. The villagers put up deck chairs in their front gardens, drank wine and shouted to each other over the fence. The evening sun picked out the Triumph's tank badge which occasionally stimulated a look of recognition from the locals as I passed through their lives.

Eventually I was back on the Great North Road but the new route robbed me of the sight of the barges at Ferrybridge and the tree lined banks by the Ferry Boat Inn. Instead concrete pillars elevated me on a long straight road that could have been anywhere, rather than the exotic and mysterious Pontefract. Things have changed a lot since I was last here, let alone since Mr Turner passed through. Now I might be prevented from finding the site of documentaries and outrage at the antics of the nation's Rockers who raced records on the jukebox into the small hours. I was in search of 'the place of ruin of many a poor young boy', as the song goes.

OVER THE TOP

The road was open and the sky blue as the three Terriers made their way north. The contemporary report of the Gaffer's Gallop records:-

> *After lunch at Boroughbridge the trio carried themselves northwards again and ambled gently along for 70 miles before calling a halt for a cuppa all round.*

They were heading for the neck of Britain, the narrowest part of the nation. Paradoxically, the feeling is one of vastness in these wide open spaces. To the right was the horse racing town of Thirsk where the squire insisted that the railway station be moved three miles out of town, compelling those the Duke of Wellington feared would be 'encouraged to move around' to an inconvenient walk. To the left, the Yorkshire Dales and right in the middle, the fertile Vale of York; this maybe a thrifty county but these acres yield vast wealth and they still sell brogues and tweeds in sensible numbers, seemingly unaffected by the advent of coffee bars, drape suits and much else.

Riding in their customary perfect formation the Gaffers pulled off the Great North Road and leant gently into the wide roundabout at the famous Scotch Corner. Behind the shimmering ivy clad walls of the Scotch Corner Hotel, the grandparents of today's local landowners had witnessed the occasional passing of a lumbering Leyland truck, bracing itself for its lonely grind over the Pennines. Identical motorcycles one, two and three with riders uniformed in smart new Barbour suits followed by a swanky Sunbeam-Talbot caused a glance over the top of their *Farmers Weekly*, but no more.

The Great North Road fell into the distance as the Gaffers now headed due west on the rising A66. It was a lonely old road with only the fells and tumbling streams for company. The map shows steep climbs and high peaks. Nearby Arkengarthdale sports no fewer than four summits that in the failing October light looked imposing. The road continues to climb until there is no shelter on the tops where the fresh wind blows all the year round. Could this really be the same country that created the London smog that would be gathering in the choking gaslight world of the capital a mere 350 miles to the south? That cocktail of pollutants that engulfed the capital's streets and had blighted the quality of life from the era of Sherlock Holmes to *Dixon of Dock Green*. Mr Turner leant into the strong northern wind that buffeted him. Who in their right mind would leave the rural communities through which he had travelled and trade it in for the city's choking streets and crowded tenement blocks? Many it would seem.

Britain was heading for the 'never had it so good' era of the last Edwardian Prime Minister, Harold 'Super Mac' Macmillan. The phrase roughly translates into 'you've never done so much shopping'. Affluence would leap from the silver screen and into the High Street in no time. People wanted and the young seemed to want more and were prepared to pay the price for it. The desire for affluence, which initially at least broadly equated to possession of consumer goods, led to the belief that no longer were they

> kindred....bound together throughout their lives in a comprehensive system of rights and duties...(and that)... as a result the social changes set in motion by the industrial revolution, relatives (had)...become separated from each other.

At a time when all the pitfalls of the passage from childhood to adulthood via puberty lay in wait, there was the added burden of being a consumer. The previous generation's luxury became the next generation's necessity. As we consumed, the family evening was less about the relationship with those in close physical proximity, but those on the television following the Coronation induced a sales boom of TV sets. Lord Reith had to decide how to entertain three million of them every night. He spoke sincerely of the BBC's:-

> Moral responsibility - moral in the broadest way; intellectual and ethical...

For better or worse, *I Claudius* gave way to Hughie Green and a quiz show called *Double Your Money*. People were now interested in money and would do anything to get it. Thus Hughie plucked from obscurity the porter or dockhand, now pressed uncomfortably into his ill-fitting suit to face the questions. A nervous wife stood proudly behind her husband fingering her plastic pearls in the hope that the right answer might yield a new toaster or some other electrical appliance. Fifteen minutes of fame leads to an easier breakfast and reverence from the neighbours. These were the thoughts of the many who heard Mr Turner's passing, but their hearts were not in another ordinary fell-land night of the 7th of October, 1953.

Once passed Brough it was easier going for the Terriers as they rumbled downhill passed Great Ormside and into Penrith. It was an evening just like that in Exeter two days previously. The town was waiting to go home; but for how long would Mum and Dad's cramped house with its shoehorned grandparent sleeping in the parlour contain restless souls? Twenty years of the 'bright lights' of Penrith or Exeter were more than enough.

The collective restlessness of a whole generation, led to the transfer of domestic tension in the home to grave melancholy at the railway platform. High drama was now played out as the Tannoy announced the departure of the iron monster for London. The bus depot witnessed many weeping families as they implored some wayward son that there were no cheaper rents in Bermondsey than in nearby Morecambe. Just what was so good about elsewhere and would it live up to its depiction on the silver screen? For Mr Turner's family it was very different. His daughters would go to private schools in Switzerland, hardly the subject matter of the British New Wave of gritty film making. In the other Britain, children would cling to their mothers' legs at railway stations and bus depots; they never liked to see adults cry. To young eyes it was all so incomprehensible. To Mr Turner's generation it was growing proof of the dangers of the breakdown of the old order.

Once out of the lives of the people of Penrith there followed a fast ride along the straight A6 towards Carlisle. As a devoted, if largely absent, father Mr Turner would let his family invade his thoughts. His biography records:-

Edward's children adored him and considered him a wonderful father......one February he taped a whole series of sto ries for his children before he went off to America, one for every day of his absence.

There was no need to do this prior to the Gaffers' Gallop. His first had only arrived the previous April when he was the tender age of fifty-two. He was cock-a-hoop and ensured that his family were never acquainted with the grimy real life difficulties that were a more accurate picture of this 'settled and gentle time'.

THE HOUSE OF THE RISING SUN

I continued heading north on an eerily empty main road recalling the tales of woe that surrounded an anonymous café bar, an old juke box and packs of 'hooligans' the media re-named 'rockers'. The newspaper men claim to have been sat there one night as the juke box set in motion the chords of Hilton Valentine as two bikes left Squires café car park. They had four minutes and nineteen seconds to race a set distance and return before the song finished. Those left behind in the café heard a singer, 'as deep and gravely as the north-east English coal town of Newcastle that spawned him' howl:-

> *There is a house in New Orleans*
> *They call the Rising Sun*
> *And it's been the ruin of many a poor boy*
> *And God I know I'm one*

The lads on the bikes had been stuck in some factory in Leeds all day and hardly able to wait for this moment to arrive. It was an old people's world with their cautious advice ringing in their ears at home and at work. Now they were free.

The bikes shot through sedate villages with their stone pubs draped in horse brasses, and whatever the advert says, there is more to life than Tetley's Beer. They know. They had heard it in the songs: songs of elsewhere. Elsewhere was where leather jackets and blue denim jeans were not frowned upon.

Clutch in, down a gear as the road twists.

> *My mother was a tailor*
> *Sewed my new blue jeans,*
> *My father was a gambling man*
> *Down in New Orleans*

Passed the old oak where the road was still damp from the evening shower and then wind the throttle back to the stop with the heart racing, megaphones deafening and the vibration of Triumph's hottest bike drumming up through the skinny seat.

Working lads will get their fun, which has to be cheap, wherever they can. Gathering on the edge of town in the summer's evening breeze, kicking their heels until someone emerges over the brow of a hill to issue a challenge. They cannot pronounce 'disenfranchised', even if they know what it means, but it applies to them.

In the mid-sixties entertainers were nice; Tommy Steel knew his place and girls screamed at The Beatles. They were working class but never lippy and their music was moderate and for mass consumption. None of them spoke of a family's eternal struggle against social injustice and the pitfalls that exist for those who were born on the wrong side of town. What the rockers identified with beyond Carnaby Street and the BBC bubble, was the work bell ringing railroad life of black blues singers who'd had it tough too. For these lads and for the majority of people, life was more about outside toilets and *The Sound Of Music* than the so-called 'swinging sixties'.

Down the lane towards the Great North Road that leads to somewhere else as the slag heaps of South Yorkshire and silhouetted winding gear come into view in the setting sun. Were the riders condemned to follow their fathers down the mines? It was all a long way from Yoko Ono's art gallery and the only Tariq Ali around here kept whippets like everyone else. What exactly did the self-appointed social commentators of the sixties know of this world? Far less than Georgia Turner, the sixteen year old daughter of a coal miner from Middlesborough, Kentucky, USA. On the night of the 15th of September, 1937 she entered the house of Tilman Cable and was recorded singing *Rising Sun Blues*. Had that recording never been made it would have been lost for ever and a bunch of unlikely lads from the industrial north-east prevented from scorching a line of white heat through a very conformist mid-sixties pop charts. From the land of Northern Lights and iron-span bridges came Eric Burdon and The Animals. They took this ancient ballad of tragedy around a brothel, gambling den, jailhouse or house of detention for syphilis sufferers, depending on your interpretation and the result was, 'as if they had connected the ancient tune to a live wire'. Analysis of lyrics was for another generation yet to arrive and brutally, a different class of teenager. What spoke to the blokes gathered at Squires or the Ace Café was just how right it all sounded: echoes of the blues, reference to a life of chance and a wanderer's trunk. When you have spent all day in a steel mill you do not want to listen to songs about some bronzed Californian surf dude surrounded by doe-eyed beauties.

As time went by the BBC sent documentary makers up the Great North Road and what they came back with caused veteran broadcaster Cliff Michelmore to shake his head in disbelief. They had been to Squires Café, stuck a camera in the faces of the clientele who obliged by putting on a bit of a show. The public's relationship with motorcycles was never an easy one: 'The Suicide Club' rang out the *Daily Mirror*. They loved it really.

The Final mile:-

Now the only thing a gambler needs
Is a suitcase and a trunk
And the only time he's satisfied
Is when he's on a drunk

Alan Price's fingers danced across the keyboard of his Vox Continental organ. The notes whirl and fall in confusion. What's this? No happy ending! Hilton's chords are being whipped up as Chas Chandler's solemn base anchors the song to its roots in sin and misery. They sure don't do things the way Cliff Richard used to.

The lads are flat out; they just will not take advice these days:-

Oh mother tell your children
Not to do what I have done
Spend your life in sin and misery
In the house of the Rising Sun

After being ahead through the lanes, there's no way he will give up the lead now. It means going into that corner a bit too fast, leaning it a bit too far. Perhaps he will get a slap on the back for this one and let's face it he will never get one for 'coming good'. These were their rites of passage in a world of tough guy values and miner's clubs full of slow talking amateur boxers. These values could suffocate you if it is Carnaby Street you want.

Well I got one foot on the platform
The other foot on the train
I'm going back to New Orleans
To wear that ball and chain

The hypnotic drumbeat plays on as the bikes are ready to burst and Price literally squeezes a shimmering wall of sound out of the organ. The village, the traffic lights, death or glory:-

Well there is a house in New Orleans
They call the Rising Sun

It has been a long wait at the café and the old speakers did their best as the stylus edges towards the centre of the 45. They can hear the snarling bikes as they round the corner.

And it's been the ruin of many a poor boy
And God I know I'm one

They are impressed in the car park. At the chippy opposite they shake their heads in bewilderment.

The dog-eared photographs of these nights exist in family albums and occasionally bike magazines. Young toughs looking up the road, schoolboys looking on, a bloke on a BSA putting on his gloves. It is unposed and they had no idea that it would become the stuff of legend. Some still go to the café regularly even though they are drawing their pensions: some never made it.

I pulled into a windswept service station a few short miles from Squires Café. The only other vehicle on the forecourt was a Land Rover with a horsebox. I could see the horsey owner in the shop in vigorous conversation with the heavily made up girl on the till. I strolled in as horsey stormed out and the girl greeted me with "she 'ad a face like a slapped arse". We are in Yorkshire now and everything within the county boundary is about right and everything without is wrong. So long as you remember that you will be all right. The horsebox darted passed the window, which drew further comment to wit, "daft bitch" whereon she returned to pummelling her chewing gum once more. With her words ringing in my ears I rode the final miles before pulling off into the winding lanes and went in search of Squires Café.

The great thing about legends is that you can always add a bit on as you go along. Which hoodlum really was responsible for the first record race, if they ever happened at all, as some cynics question? I can reveal that they had innocent beginnings, thanks to everyone's favourite bobby, Dixon of Dock Green. On the evening of January the 14th, 1961 nineteen year old Nobby from Willesden, North London sat at home with his Mum, enthralled by George Dixon's latest story:-

"Evenin' all…..y'know, if I've got a bee in my bonnet about one particular thing, I suppose it's road safety."

It is iconic for its innocence. George Dixon was a proper copper, the kind human rights lawyers hate. When he strode under the gaslight to greet the nation he spoke of his concern for young motorcyclists. And he was about to depart from long standing broadcasting etiquette and name a real place as the scene of a crime and from that moment on the legend was born.

"Coffee bar cowboys. These young 'erbs who hang out at the caffs with their flash bikes and their girls. What's the local caff Andy?"
"The Ace."

"That's the place. Might be an idea to pop up there some time and see what goes on."

For Nobby, the Ace was his local café and he heard a youthful Jess Conrad plant the evil seed:-

"Just up the roundabout and down the hill. Put on a record – see if we can get back before it ends."

From here Nobby moved seamlessly to the pages of the *Willesden Chronicle* where under the headlines, 'Up Up Up, Went The Speedometer' his great day, in court was recorded for posterity.

Pacing up and down one of London's less famous legal addresses at Willesden Magistrates, Mr George Schindler, prosecuting, had a seed of his own to plant, in the minds of Their Worships:-

It is perhaps significant that on that particular night there was a programme on television which dealt with youngsters on motorcycles at the Ace Café. Whether that has any bearing on the case I'm not prepared to say.

Too late. Seed planted, Nobby got a £35 fine and the Wurlitzers around the country started doing a roaring trade.

I had not been back to Squires Café since one of the Rockers Reunion nights in the mid-eighties. Remarkably, British bikes never went out of fashion even for those who could not remember the sixties, because when something is right it does not need changing. 'Untainted by technology' rings the advert today for Royal Enfield in America. And it is in America that an entirely new generation have discovered British bikes in a big way. As I was doing the Gaffers' Gallop, a rash of documentaries were being made about American bikers who were not even alive when the last of Mr Turner's Triumphs rolled off the production line. First up was Hooligan Films who interviewed British Bikers in Los Angeles. Incredibly they look like the kids in the old photographs of Squires, the Ace , and the rest. One interviewee tells us:-

Real bikes are built in garages by nineteen year old kids who have three hundred bucks to spend not three thousand.

Manufacturers want to make self-reliance extinct. So much technology makes you totally dependant on a franchised dealer with a diagnostic computer. The motorcycle, symbol of freedom, becomes a vehicle of exploitation for a garagiste with an easy smile. But in Los Angeles they have got it sussed:-

Why do you reengineer something that was never a problem fifty years ago?

The last thing I remember about Squires was a 7ft foot plastic Teddy Boy outside, but he was nowhere to be seen tonight and neither was anyone else as the place was like a ghost town. Not at all like the Rocker's Reunion of way back, when I had stood in the chip shop opposite as bikes thundered by, chrome alight under the streetlights. I spotted an old boy in the queue, goggles up, his craggy features turned to the bikes outside. Now he really could have been an original with his leathers scuffed at the elbow and knee, bearing the patina of age now moulded to fit his ageing frame. *Très chic* and in Yorkshire to boot!

As I rode through the village they had little idea that in Southern California, a film company was adding the finishing touches to *Britown*, a documentary about a British bike mechanic called Meatball from down town Anahiem. Meatball builds Triumphs the old way, rides motocross like Steve McQueen, plays in a rock 'n' roll band and speaks from the heart:-

> *I can still remember the smell of my Dad's Triumph when he would shut it off, it had a weird smell you know, it was hot…Once in a while a bike will come into the shop and I will smell that smell again and go, man.*

He would have enjoyed the Rocker's Reunions of the mid-eighties, if he had been around. But in California 'it's not so much about livin' in the past as takin' the past forward' so it just does not matter that you weren't there in the sixties, eighties or whenever, which is a real pisser for people who bang on about the Paris riots every eighth year of the decade.

Like the VW campervan, there are some designs that should go on for ever because they can not be bettered and every generation has its percentage of the discerning who wonder why modern manufacturers can not make something more erm…interesting? Triumph certainly tried when they made the modern Thunderbird. Their brochure read:-

In the 1950s Britain rebelled

Thin on technical information yet it got the message across. By now I was too tired to rebel, and unable to find my way around another bypass that had been added since I was last here, which to all intents and purposes diverted me from where I wanted to be. Everywhere seemed flooded and only a solitary biker emerged through the gathering mist. It seemed a long time since up to four thousand motorcyclists would gather on a balmy summer's evening. And with that thought in mind I took the roundabout and headed 'out of town', even if it was only a village in Yorkshire.

I was soon at the traffic lights on the cross roads in the tiny village of Cawood on the River Ouse. Period terraced houses: old tenements that used to belong to barge hands line the street and are so narrow that you can nearly shake hands over the road from the top floors. The last time I was here there was a British bike at every corner and the rumbling brought the locals out to look in admiration remembering when…

That was over twenty years ago. I was on my own tonight and without any rumbling. Compared to Mr Turner's Triumphs, my own looks like a tenor but sings like a eunuch. Now dangerous drivers say, "sorry mate, I didn't hear you".

The lights changed and I moved off, easing up at the swing bridge. Beneath me the deep Ouse swelled as it surged passed the wooden stumps of the old bridge before charging to the sea.

I watched the sky turn dark blue as the moon came up over the 12th century church and leant on one of the bowstring girders that support the battleship deck of the bridge. Since 1872 a swing span has given precedence to vessels and it took an Act of Parliament to replace the bridge keeper that occupied the wooden hut halfway across with cameras. They were my only company until I was joined by a lone cyclist who balanced adjacent to one of the girders and puffed on his pipe while surveying the scene. A curlew flew over the top of the poplars that surround the vicarage and darted out across the flood, drumming as it skimmed the surface. A couple more puffs on his pipe and the cyclist turned back into the village and I out across the plain. Stones and debris had been washed onto the road. It was like this for the next twenty miles during which time I did not see a single other vehicle. Finally I turned the top of the road on which I grew up, promising to spare you from excessive sentiment. I pulled up and sat down to a meal of pheasant and spring ale followed by bilberry pie hand picked from around the White Horse of Kilburn. Some writer once wrote:

Home is the place where you spend your childhood trying to leave and the rest of your life trying to return to.

Then my folks told me that they had doubled the sponsorship I had raised from my ambitious but ultimately ineffective methods. That writer was right.

Mr Turner was well ahead of me now, but then his Mum and Dad weren't waiting for him in the village of Wheldrake just outside York, with some good old fashioned home cooking, as mine were.

I retired to my old bedroom lined with photographs of epic and not so epic journeys undertaken twenty odd years ago. All was quiet as the curtains swayed in a gentle breeze and then I was fast asleep.

THE CROWN AND MITRE

All three Terriers were thrumming along nicely on the long straight into Carlisle. Like Leamington Spa and Exeter before that, the riders witnessed the drawing to a close of an unremarkable day in a provincial town. If there was anything to report about Thursday the 8th of October, 1953 it has been lost to the passage of time. One can safely say that people went to work, went shopping and whatever they bought was not vacuum packed in plastic. And then they went home; I like to think without dropping any litter. As with Exeter, the locals crammed onto the Corporation bus with their daily papers, safe in the knowledge that the transport system was integrated and did not indulge in the modern fashion for delivering you after your connection has left. The whistle of the night train blew because I have tried to paint a sentimental picture of this as an era of a content population, living in country cottages led by leaders so remote that the populace was childishly ignorant of their faults.

Mr Turner had covered 246 miles in 6¾ hours. Most in Carlisle who witnessed his passing were themselves happy simply to be in work and not at war. Envy, status, angst and celebrity devotion did not trouble this generation even if they did not all really live in country cottages. What they did however, was contribute to a survey on national spending thereby leaving an unequivocal testimony to what a sensible lot they were when compared to latter day litter-bugs.

The Office for National Statistics survey on family spending tells us far more about the reality of these spiritual days when the Queen reigned through:-

A series of ritual affirmations of the moral values necessary to a well- governed and good society.

When considered some 50 years later one commentator concluded:-

We earn more, own more and have the world at our feet thanks to cheap air travel, (but) our lives are not nearly so much fun...

Today we spend more on gambling than fresh vegetables. It is not recorded what Mr Turner would have said about this but I just thought I would throw it in as a cheap poke at modern living after trying to masquerade as a fair and balanced commentator of our times.

The three Terriers went in search of the Crown and Mitre Hotel in Carlisle and felt the draft of the Celtic influence from over the border with Scotland. The hotel stands on the site of the old Crown and Mitre Inn, which dated back to the Jacobite rebellion. Edwardian in style, sandstone in construction and huge in dimension, one is under no illusion that this pile, with its ninety-four rooms situated next to Carlisle Cathedral, was another hand picked venue to keep the choosy Mr Turner content. Even so he felt he had occasion to berate the planners:-

Why aren't we scheduled to do more miles in a day?

His skills as a former racer had led him to set a cracking pace throughout the journey. Confidently he continued:-

This is just so easy it's plain silly.

However, as the contemporary report from *MotorCycling* magazine dared to point out:-

Four fine and dry days in a row could hardly have been foreseen by old Moore himself, and this particular dispensation of fates has meant instead of three tired men peeling off their machines at the end of the day and making tracks for the nearest bathrooms, three exuberant excursionists are ribbing the planners for cramping their style.

Cramped as he may have felt his riding style had become, the hotel was some compensation even if he did not enjoy a homemade tea of bilberry pie. In fact, if Mr Turner ever had somewhere he could call home, it would have been in the years immediately following the Gaffers' Gallop. Thereafter hotels would once again feature large in his life. The start of this evolution to his hotel sentence began with the courtship of Mr Turner's second wife and has a distinctly romantic tinge, as you might expect. Not instantly recognised by his staff as an 'old smoothy', they may have been surprised to hear that on a trip to New Zealand he had struck up an acquaintance with a beauty queen waitress who was about to start working her way through Europe. The queen in question was called Shirley and she accompanied him back from New Zealand following one of his many business trips abroad. Sadly they lost touch, but Mr Turner was able to call on the good offices of his customers, the New Zealand Police to make discreet enquiries and they were reunited. Mr Turner sent her an air ticket and suggested that they meet in Rome. There he proposed to her and they were married at St George's Church in Hanover Square, London on the 19th of July 1952. Mr Turner's best man from his first wedding carried out the same function. Happily, children started to arrive and a seat convenient for the Turner family had to be found. These were invariably country piles in extensive grounds where his young wife had two daughters to look after, usually on her own. This prompted the observation from Shirley that:-

All I seem to do is sit here and watch the newscasters grow old.

On Mr Turner's return from any of his innumerable trips abroad, he would eat the meal Shirley had prepared, in his own room watching television as if his bachelor days had not been brought to a happy end. At approaching sixty he was very set in his ways and Shirley rapidly realised that she would never change him.

Paternally, Mr Turner appears to have been flawless. He knew his daughters' dress sizes off by heart and they, by contrast, benefited from his trips abroad. When at home a routine emerged that was typical of the times. Shirley would stay in the kitchen and prepare the Sunday lunch whilst Mr Turner took his daughters for a morning walk. This included stopping to pat 'Old George', a retired carthorse before strolling to the humpback bridge over the stream. On their return, Mr Turner was off to visit friends for pre lunch drinks. This left the girls in a large house in which it was easy to get lost. They often explored, as children will, happening upon a fascinating array of multicoloured bottles in their father's drinks cabinet. From there they would creep into his study and admire the portrait of their father in his Merchant Navy uniform. Another portrait of him as a younger man hung on the stairs, having been painted by Mr Turner's talented sister. The third portrait was of their father's first wife Marion who had died in a car crash. They were small girls on a starry eyed adventure about the ramparts of their father's manor. The silent portraits stared down upon them, as they were oblivious to their significance during their venture into their father's other life. That significance would become apparent as they matured into women. Mr Turner's second daughter, who visited Meriden on the eve of its destruction, was christened Charmian Marion Turner. But for now they gently closed the door behind them and followed the distant echo of their mother serving Sunday lunch.

The physical isolation of those rural piles became too much for Shirley and she and Mr Turner reached a compromise whereby the family seat was moved closer to the bright lights of London. This required Mr Turner to live out of his suitcase in a hotel during the week, travelling home at weekends. His biography recalls:-

> From Edward's point of view however, it turned out to be a retrograde step that placed him at a disadvantage. He was now isolated from his wife and young family throughout the week and had to take up residence in the Leofric Hotel, Coventry. No matter how good the hotel, it still had that impersonal atmosphere about it, to remind him of his 'double life'; with his working colleagues during the week, and with his wife and children at weekends....he began to feel a stranger in his own house, especially as he did not receive the welcome he might expect at the weekends.

As he climbed the stairs of the Crown and Mitre, hotels had no negative connotations. The difficulties with Shirley had not yet been encountered and whilst at fifty-two, it was hardly all ahead of him, he clearly enjoyed fatherhood and had much to look forward to. Or so he thought.

UP TO THE BORDER

I gently drifted through Wheldrake and cast a glance at the playground in front of my old school, noting that children appear far better behaved today than they used to be.

I was on the road and on my own once more, making my way north. In the distance the Yorkshire Wolds rise up out of the Vale of York offering vast fields from the Humber to the Moors, to the sun. One can leave the Wolds for half a century and return to find that little has changed. About them the world carries on at its usual pace but if the locals want to get away from it all, it is to the Wolds that they head. These qualities were not lost on their most famous son, Edward Lord Halifax, the Foreign Secretary who tried to broker peace with the man with the moustache from Austria. His biography recounts:-

> *This vast county seems to possess an existence independent of the rest of England, and to constitute a separate world of its own. It is a world of varied and entrancing beauty…the Vale of York, the chalky Wolds, to Edward the very essence of Yorkshire, where a man could ride sixty miles across the great crescent of chalk hills from Flamborough to the Humber, and look down on the villages lying in their folds, on the flowers, and on churches among the dark firs by the streams.*

I spent most of my childhood looking at the Wolds from a classroom. Like his Lordship, I was forever trying to get away from it all but perhaps my burdens did not compare with trying to reason with Hitler.

I rode over the flooded River Wharfe and headed north towards Boroughbridge. The White Horse was on my right and the Pennines to my left as I wound my way through a patchwork of fields before taking the sharp right into the market square in Boroughbridge. I parked beside the well for the obligatory photo shoot pulling up alongside a group of pensioners in cagoules receiving a lecture on architecture. The day was breezy and quiet and I felt a little uneasy positioning the bike, secure in the knowledge that the lecturer knew chapter and verse of the particular byelaw that I had just breached. Happily, I failed to attract any attention from them as the wind blew off the moors, across the vale and ruffled their silver locks.

When the prestigious American magazine *National Geographic* ran a profile on the area it wrote:-

> *So who are the Northerners, these English who feel so different from other English…suspecting that in the South a more soft, more effete more predatory England has fattened upon Northern inventiveness, upon Northern sweat… believing themselves tougher, friendlier, blunter but more honest?*

There is certainly a more practical view of life around here, which makes it difficult for those of us who have left these wide open spaces to readjust to the questionable benefits of the suburban idyll.

On leaving Boroughbridge I too joined the Great North Road. I ticked off the lines of longitude as I headed north. The signs for Scarborough came up first, host of Oliver's Mount motorcycle races. It was here that I first spied a national institution. A breed of individual who lived by their motorcycles having been metamorphosised from an ageing rocker to 'the last of the blue bloods, a greaser boy' as the song goes. In an age of something called 'glam rock' there existed through resistance and ritual a rather dangerous body of men who arrogantly refused to move with the times. They caught the curious attention of a band called Jethro Tull whose little ditty mapped out the trials of those *Too Old To Rock And Roll But Too Young To Die*. You may have met him, recognising him by his efforts to convince you that he has seen the light and you have sold out. Wearing the same leather jacket and hairstyle whilst his friends marry and wheel their bikes out for the last time before they are placed in the small ads. No one has managed to get this lot to rhyme but even so there are a lot of embarrassed stiffs in suits who once thought like this. One was going to 'live to ride' and never get married or mortgaged. As American journalist Peter Egan recalls:-

> *It all started in the late sixties, when I was languishing in college. Back in those days I thought that the three finest things in the world were a Nikon camera, a Martin guitar, and a Triumph motorcycle. (I was trying to shun materialism but hadn't quite got the hang of it).I was certain that if you could latch onto those three items your earthly needs would be forever complete. Sure you might need some clothes, a place to sleep, an occasional meal and a few Jack Kerouac novels, but those were all minor, secondary considerations.*

The hero of our song could have identified with these sentiments, but his life was about to take a dramatic turn:-

> *So the old rocker gets out his bike*
> *to make a ton before he takes his leave*
> *upon the A1 by Scotch Corner just like it used to be…*
> *and he hits the trunk road doing around 120*
> *with no room left to brake*

And I too was up on the A1 by Scotch Corner, trying to catch a whiff of hot oil that may have hung in the atmosphere following the passing of the old greaser or even Mr Turner, but it was not to be. The road over the Pennines as taken by Mr Turner turned out to be blocked by floods and fallen trees. Perhaps it was just a test that fate had thrown for Mr Turner to assess whether they still made motorcyclists as resilient as they used to be. I would not be put off and would meet Mr Turner via a different route. However, I had no complaint about heading to the borders through Tyneside, and who would? County Durham, that land of Prince Bishops, came round first, castles, cathedrals and dark brooding moor land. And then one of the finest cities of them all, Newcastle upon Tyne. My view is not tempered by being an alumnus of this city. I am quite capable of recognising that Newcastle has suffered at the stray dog school of architecture with so many old men in a hurry and desperate to leave their mark. I offer some consolation to the locals in the form of the plight of at least one developer in the all time gangster classic *Get Carter*, who came to a sticky end at the foot of one such piece of modern architecture.

I travelled on the ring road over its industrial buildings, scrap yards, wasteland and tributaries to the Tyne. Then ahead of me was the sign for the A696 that would take me out and over the Northumbria National Park. I swung off the ring road and followed the finest twisting motorcycling road on the face of the earth. Within moments of leaving Newcastle I was in beautiful wilderness; please God do not let them spoil it. I passed through Ponteland and out to Higham Dykes and into a land of small stone hamlets, bridges over tumbling streams and shops selling vast quantities of wellies. The road started to climb, gradually at first as fields gave way to moorland. Then from Otterburn onwards the heavens opened and the scent of pine gave way to that of peat bog. The cloud engulfed the wind farms as I pressed on to the final peak and then I saw an upright granite rock into which was boldly engraved the word: 'Scotland'. Beside that was the figure of a solitary bagpiper. I was seconds away from the border.

IT'S EASY ON A TRIUMPH

Or so ran the series of cartoon adverts that Triumph commissioned in the fifties. It was a time when demand outstripped supply and the company simply wanted to keep the brand in the eye of a patient and expectant public. In one scene a Bentley chases a Triumph as its rider and pillion race towards Gretna Green, the capital of marriage ceremonies for runaway couples. Both the rider and pillion girl look thrilled to be in the lead under which the caption reads 'It's easy on a Triumph'.

If Mr Turner ever considered Gretna Green as a romantic setting for his and Shirley's union it is not recorded, and Shirley's possible response is perhaps best left to the imagination.

Mr Turner was in the foyer of the Crown and Mitre, preparing for the short ride to the Scottish border. But he was not crossing that border until he had made his religious call to his 'little factory in England' for the usual run down of the production figures. The lady at the end of the phone was his secretary, the redoubtable Nan Plant. By all accounts Nan was a star. Many in the factory took advantage of her diplomatic advice when invited to an audience with Mr Turner, or received the nod from her when he would grace the shop floor with his presence. Her dedication to Triumph was beyond question and she would often go into work on Saturdays so Mr Turner could shout at her as much as he liked, cooling off on Sundays and giving the rest of the staff an easier time on Monday.

On the morning of the 9th of October she found Mr Turner in a very agreeable frame of mind as he prepared to take his motorcycles over the border. That border did not feel like a political border although culturally there is a change. One side of the River Sark they speak this way and on the other side, that way. But after a war in which all Scottish regiments fought with their customary valour, one could sit in one's cottage or wherever, safe in the knowledge that the Union of England, Scotland, Wales and Northern Ireland was still intact. The symbol of that bond was the Stone of Scone, which lay under the Coronation chair in Westminster Abbey. All those with the right to govern sat on it at their coronation, when it gave out a low groan if the incumbent were the real thing or remained silent if not. Or put another way:-

> *The Scots shall govern,*
> *And the sceptre sway,*
> *Where'er the stone, they find,*
> *And it's dread sound obey.*

Not long before the Gaffers' Gallop, a group of law students from Glasgow University took it back under cover of darkness and planted it in Arbroath Abbey. Then they gave it back, entente cordial was restored, the Gaffers were guaranteed a safe passage and in time one of the students was made a Queen's Counsel.

The news hound from *MotorCycling* magazine was scribbling the following words in the foyer of the Crown and Mitre when he heard the bikes burst into life and pull away:-

> *Nothing short of a calamity will rob the Terriers and their jockeys the joy of achieving, by lunchtime tomorrow, average speeds and petrol consumption figures far better than the most optimistic wishful thinking could have produced.*

Stabbing a full stop in his notebook, he scrambled into the last car to pull out and off they chased after the now irrepressible Gaffers who had wound back their throttles.

Mr Turner rode on alone. To his right the fields were punctuated with thistles, lined with barbed wire fences with drift wood posts that held back occasional flocks of sheep. He leant into the sharp wind that blows up the Solway Firth as the first signs for Scotland came up.

The staff of the Gretna Chase Hotel could hear the rumbling down the road for some time. They were not busy, for the numbers of people staying in a hotel following a marriage ceremony in austerity Britain were few. The hotel was on the A74 and wore about it the dowdy look of a building too close to traffic and dust for comfort.

Moments later a car careered around the corner and drove over the bridge screeching to a halt on the Scottish side of the river bank. The news hound leapt out and set up his cameras. The bikes could be heard revving in the distance as they made their way over the last half a mile of England. They eased up before the Gretna Chase and the staff watched from the window as the fat one in the middle manoeuvred himself to the fore. Three men in black graciously growled their way into view and over the bridge. Alec Masters was on the right and Bob Fearon, the left. Behind the Sunbeam Talbot and bringing up the rear was Colin Swaisland, the ESSO cameraman on the 500cc Speed Twin. Proudly in the middle and very much to the fore as ever, was Mr Turner. It was exactly 9 am on Friday the 9th of October, 1953. Mr Turner was seconds away from crossing the border.

THE PHILOSOPHER

After hours of climbing, the bike crested the brow of the hill and I passed from England and into Scotland. The landscape now fell beneath me to reveal a panorama of pristine countryside stretching from the Cheviot Hills to Upper Tweedale in the distance. I rode in to the car park where the piper was playing to an audience of mature Japanese businessmen and their very young wives.

Scotland has for the time being, decided to remain part of Britain where it won the country the title of the 'workshop of the world'. A contemporary history book reminds a new generation that

Scottish industry had...once illuminated the heavier end of the world economy.

Scotland has compensated itself for this loss by increasing the size of its civil service just like they have in England. By contrast the piper was earning his money today. He ran from one side of the road to the other as tourists came and went. Never did he squeeze more than a few bars out of *Amazing*

Grace or *Speed Bonny Boat* before the obligatory photograph was taken and off they disappeared over the brow of the hill.

I was joined by the genial piper under the clouds sporting their leaden tinge. For now he was free of jokes about sporrans, which I felt was a pretty poor way of treating an ancient culture. But the Scots are a pragmatic lot and the piper confided that he was looking forward to global warming to extend his six months on the border to eight. And then he looked to the heavens and exclaimed, "Aye, but aah didnae reckon on this bloody weather".

Beside my bike, the piper obliged and played me into Scotland and so I took a photograph of him like the tourist I am. That the bike and I were there at all owed much to my generous sponsor, Scotoiler, who kindly sent me the mechanism that keeps my chain lubricated which was essential during this particularly wet week. How the Scotoiler came into being is typical of Scottish ingenuity that had once been widespread amongst the ancestors of all those civil servants. The story goes that inventor Fraser Scott, never really saw himself as an inventor but a man of romance. To prove his alpha male credentials he made the trip from Glasgow to Manchester to see the lady in his life by way of a Norton 850 Commando. By the time of his arrival lesser men would have been good for nothing. If he wasn't passed it, his chain invariably was. Sick of oiling that chain whilst the rose between his teeth wilted, he invented an automatic chain oiler and the wilting era was brought to an end and bikers everywhere gained something of a spring in their step.

I let the bike roll down the hill as I put her in gear and started her up. Scotland fell beneath my wheels as I passed a lamp post which provided a perch for a buzzard that indifferently witnessed my passing. The road followed Jed Water for miles as it twisted its way into Jedburgh whose ghostly ruined abbey welcomes the traveller as he rounds the corner. I passed anonymously through Newtown St Boswells, a town breaking for lunch and quietly going about its business.

Miles of green countryside and dripping woodland separated isolated villages as I wound ever northward. Again the clouds turned heavy and grey and the rain ever more persistent as I entered Lauder. The town was empty as my tyres splashed through the puddles on the High Street. In the town square, outside the bakers I spotted the functional lines of an old Royal Enfield motorcycle before pulling into the petrol station. As I filled her up I could hear a rumbling down the road and the Royal Enfield rider pulled in behind me. I nodded to him but got no response and so I paid no more

attention to him and went into the petrol station. On returning, the silver
bearded biker was a little more talkative.

"Just two pounds" he said replacing the nozzle. "That's all I'll pay for a
weeks transport. And you?"

"A bit more".

"Aye, ya will on that thing" he said, nodding towards the Triumph. It
should have killed the conversation but old silver locks hung around.

"Where ya headin'?"

"John O'Groats."

"Aye ma sister lives there, ya must give my regards to Mary."

It turned out that silver locks drove the local bus and was clocking off
for the day.

"The pay's crap but aah couldnae live in London. Instead I drive some
lovely people around the beautiful borders. It could be worse." Suddenly he
became more animated.

"Only this morning I was driving by the river when a buzzard flew
alongside me for two or three minutes and we both had eye contact with
each other. Tell me, what other job could offer me that?" I could not.

"Aye, I could leave this for a city and the promise of a better life but you and
I know better" he said squinting up at the sky and the Scotch mist descending
all around. With that he headed back into town and I over the bridge and
lodged in my memory that I must say hello to Mary of John O'Groats.

I travelled through an empty Lauderdale that managed to instil in my
mind the prospect that this countryside would carry on forever. But I was
approaching the mighty Firth of Forth and the busy affluent capital: Edinburgh.

The crossing of an estuary is a milestone in any journey. The rocks
that are unmoved by the heaving waters are the last vestige of the land left
behind. What promise of adventure as I leave Eagle Rock on the south bank
and glance over to the north bank and Dalgety Bay.

To head this far north thirty years ago would have classed one almost
an adventurer. The countryside was wild, provisions few and television
reception non-existent. But today the M90 links Edinburgh to Perth and
the promise of estuaries crossed and mountains conquered cannot be heard
above the roar of traffic. We wonder no more what is around the next
corner; there isn't one. Loch Leven, the Bridge of Earn and the Firth of Tay
are merely a blur punctuated by aluminium road signs. If Perth had much to
commend it, I do not know: it could have been Slough for its roundabouts
are the same shape. Of course, Scotland is a nation that exists for more
than merely providing a holiday destination for sentimental Sassenachs who

have ruined their own country. But there is not much national identity to be gleaned from the town planner's obsession with the concrete kerbstone. Apparently all this is unfortunately necessary to shepherd vast numbers of tourists hither and thither.

My first Scottish holiday was many years ago. A couple of years before I arrived, the naturalist and author Gavin Maxwell penned these words, about me I suppose:-

> To me the West Highlands were composed of deer forests and hereditary chieftains...and the (hikers from the industrial cities) were regrettable interlopers upon the romantic life of the indigenous aristocracy.

I came to feel like penning similar lines about those people carriers roaring along the M90 and heading for the 'tranquillity' of the Highlands. I guess that is just the way it goes.

I was now north of Perth following the silver thread between the mountains that is the river Tay. The traffic was thicker on the single carriageway but slower as we shared the valley bottom with the railway line. The sun came out and the mountainsides closed in. Between the grind of heavy haulage the wooded hillsides sighed in silence; now it felt like Scotland.

When I was here years ago, people spoke of the coming of 'the road'. There was amongst some, in our hotel at least, a sense of foreboding. This would be the last summer where the people who were in the Highlands that year were prepared to take the mountains on their own terms. The road would bring prosperity to the locals or so the old mantra went, along with the habitual utterance of the word 'progress'. Yet everybody who had served me at a petrol station north of the border had a cockney accent. And now the road stripped the Highlands of its youth. Sure it was easy to come back, but it was easier to go in the first place. The old road had bowed to the mountains and bent with the rivers and tolerated sheep sleeping upon its surface. Moreover it brought work. It was so badly made and the prevailing belief was that the Highlands would never be entirely conquered, so teams of locals with shovels were forever mending it. The frequency of landslides gave the journey the air of a new world adventure and the road workers were a body of men whose work was never entirely complete.

As I rode along I occasionally caught a glimpse of a view that matched with some excited childhood memory from a trip I made as a schoolboy. But it was like watching the remake of an old classic: a disappointment. This was not the road on which I had travelled during my childhood or indeed that which Mr Turner had rumbled along. I was on an entirely new road built for the 'liberating' new world and devoted to 'convenience'. All of which was very commendable but simply boring. Where the old road twisted and turned and compelled the traveller to ease up for shepherds driving sheep, the new road bludgeoned its way through forests that now pass in a blur and trammelled over unseen rivers. Its dominance over the natural world is complete. But the canny Scots know that sentimental Englishmen like me holiday in their country and so they have preserved sections of the old road that run alongside the new. Sadly that road rarely came into view, as it was allowed to meander through the forests and touch the banks of the Tay. There you could hear the water and smell the pine where once this youthful writer had sat on the back seat of his parent's car watching the fly fishermen. Now foreign trucks bear down on me, and every people carrier that passed had a television set implanted into the back of the head rests.

I could not imagine any child being more excited than I when first my parents brought me here; rather worryingly I found myself muttering the sorts of comments about the inferiority of a modern childhood that they once had. But now my anticipation increased for an entirely different reason as my and Mr Turner's routes drew together once more.

Having followed the road signs pointing north to Pitlochry I was alarmed to see them all pointing south. Pitlochry was on the map but off the road and I had overshot. With my petrol running low I turned into a petrol station behind which ran the old road sporting vestiges of Highland life. Cottages with well kept gardens, a post box, a fire break in the trees and the obligatory battered Land Rover. The road served the cottages and weary travellers, taking them off the new road to the south and depositing them 100 yards further north.

In the Ballinluig petrol station a girl with the reassuringly Scottish name of Shona served me. With that I stepped out into the beautiful evening sunlight that had turned the mountainsides golden. Between the convoys of trucks I could hear the 'klee- ee' call of the oystercatcher, echoing between mountainsides as it flew in a straight line, way up in the sky. But the clang of the trucks is more reminiscent of Glen Girnaig than the sharp call of the bright billed bird. Still, at the tourist centre they do a roaring trade in wooden carvings of the bird they seldom hear anymore.

As I passed a billboard I read a headline that for once was not about the weather:-

Eighty per cent of strong cannabis consumed in the UK is home grown.

The mind boggles. Literally.

I now wanted somewhere to rest my head and turned off the main road, riding into the first campsite I came to. It was vast with static homes sporting little plastic plant pots and satellite dishes. I rode on to the camping section and lay on the grass as the oystercatchers flew overhead. Near me was a foursome in a shared tent with a brand new Range Rover. The driver would be commonly described as a 'short arse' with impossibly hairy arms and a Bermuda shirt. He was drinking wine out of a shandy glass as he walked around his clearly defined territory that stretched the length of his windbreak. On more than one occasion he gave me a hard stare as their wifeys' squawks echoed around the forest. Rab and his missus made a lot of noise, drove the Range Rover too fast, came back in the early hours of the morning and made some more noise. Slowly they started chilling out as Rab's clipped Celtic tones were applied to his very own Rastafarian impression. And then they all started chuckling but not at Rab. They were taking advantage of the efforts of those patriotic scamps Her Majesty's Ganga Growers. In the face of Scotland's withdrawal from 'the heavier end of the world economy', there was nothing left to do but get stoned as the smell of exotic substances mingled interestingly with the odour of peat bog. Rule Britannia indeed.

CATH RAON RUAIRIDH

The Gaffers followed the source of the river Esk and crossed Skipper's Bridge at Malcolm's Memorial. Miles and miles without a soul. If anything should happen up here to the solitary motorcyclist he would have to walk to some isolated hillside cottage and beg the use of a phone. This was always a disappointing endeavour as the telephone cables had long since stopped at the edge of suburban Edinburgh. And on a Sunday they do not answer any knock at the front door in any event.

It was the big one today and once through the Glasgow – Edinburgh collar at the neck of the nation, the midges are mighty, the mist intermittent and deer outnumbered people. The miles tripped away on the odometers of the Terriers registered NWD 867, NWD 868 and NWD 869. Lockerbie, Lanark and Stirling gave way to Perth, a town without roundabouts then and very much part of the Highland's micro economy with an identity all of its own. Here the Gaffers pulled into the Salutation Hotel, the first of a number of stops during a long day of twisting roads around lochs and through hamlets north of the border.

The photographer managed to snap the Gaffers sweeping around the bend from under a railway bridge. "No time to stop and they are still open!" read the caption that appeared in the following week's *MotorCycling* magazine as the Gaffers were pictured passing the Gleneagles Hotel.

Now they followed the narrow road adjacent to the river Tay. The autumn sunlight turned the surface golden as they passed stone cottages out of which wood smoke ascended skyward in the motionless air. Pitlochry heard their rumble as they passed down a high street better acquainted with meeting the needs of fishermen and stalkers than motorcyclists.

The bikes strained as they climbed between drystone walls and tumbled down trees draped with moss. To the left they could hear the roar of the River Tummel as it dropped over a series of waterfalls and swirled at the foot of the bridge. It was 3.15 pm on Friday the 9th of October, 1953. Their passing was but a moment in time, witnessed by no one as the river below continued to marshal vast quantities water to shape the gorge. Many a generation of salmon had fought their way against the current to spawn before their issue made for the open sea and many more would follow before I looked into these very waters.

In this environment of long damp miles even the staunchest motorcyclist could be forgiven for questioning whether there was a better way to travel, particularly if like Mr Turner they had sampled America's open highways and wallowing V8s. Indeed little of American culture was lost on Mr Turner. He spent up to six months a year on the continent that had the largest network of roads of any country on earth. A country where young men from New Jersey could leap in a car and take up a career in California if the magnetic force of Uncle Sam's free market happened to pull them in that direction.

The energy of an unfettered and ambitious youth helped propel America to the foremost position for the second half of the twentieth century. This coincided with the creation of a huge automotive industry and whilst Mr Turner was toiling with the lanes of Britain, a cult around life on the road was emerging from America's broad highways as the descendants of the railroad hobos were turning into the beatniks of the jazz generation.

At the same time as the Gaffer's Gallop, aspirant American writer Jack Kerouac was seeking a publisher for his account 'of the period of my life you could call my life on the road'. He had lived that life at base level, soaking up the dust of the often lonely highway and all that humanity had to offer. Whilst respectable America closed its doors for prayers and an evening meal, Kerouac's old 4.3 litre 'stove bolt' Chevrolet sung its deep mechanical ballad into the night as it made its way across the never ending American blacktop. The book that was eventually published provided a kaleidoscope of mambo music and marijuana, prison and prostitution. The 'road trip' had been brought to the attention of the wider American public. But America was far wealthier than little old Blighty that did not even start work on its first motorway until three years after the Gaffer's Gallop.

Work finally commenced on the first 8-mile stretch of our very own 'lonesome highway' on the outskirts of Preston, Lancashire on the 12th of June, 1956. The opening ceremony was marked by a junior Minister of Transport who turned the traffic lights to green to give the go ahead for a bulldozer to come crashing through a hedge whereon it promptly ran out of diesel. It was the birth of a new age.

Had this hallowed ground been available to Mr Turner he would have probably taken it as it was on his route. The thrifty Terrier would have put any car's fuel consumption to shame let alone that of a mighty Chevvy and Mr Turner's account would have been a rather more solid kaleidoscope of cigars and smoking jackets than Kerouac's hedonistic tome. Even so this could very easily have been a car borne road trip for Mr Turner had fate simply dealt him a different hand. Some years before the Gaffers' Gallop Mr Turner's name nearly became linked to one of the world's most famous marques of cars in one of the greatest curiosities in automotive history. For he, arguably one of the finest designers of motorcycles, very nearly went into business with Sir William Lyons founder of Jaguar cars and equally arguably one of the finest automotive designers. They met when Mr Turner bought Sir William's house, Woodside, near Kenilworth. By the early forties the two were in correspondence with a view to setting up a company with Sir William as chairman and Mr Turner as managing director. A contract was drawn up with both contributing £10,000 in share capital to a new company that initially intended to produce motorcycles for the war effort. It was Mr Turner who withdrew when he was tempted away by the mighty Birmingham Small Arms company whose empire included Daimler Cars.

In time Daimler approached Mr Turner to add his magic touch to their rather staid line up. Having seen the movement of peoples affected by Buick, Chevrolet and Cadillac in the United States and their appetite for simple rumbling V-8s priced to suit everyone, Mr Turner already had his own views. Sir William had by then produced the iconic Jaguar XK range with overhead cams and an enviable racing pedigree appreciated by the more discerning.

Mr Turner was having none of it and chose to question his designer, Jack Wicks. His biography recounts:-

After some thought, Jack suggested a Cadillac engine would be as good a starting point as any, whereupon Edward, with a smile, produced a Cadillac manual and spare parts list from a drawer in his desk.

The ebb and flow of the tide of history was in America's direction and Mr Turner knew it. The Turner V8 powered Daimler Dart sports car that emerged was in many ways Britain's very own Corvette Stingray, with its lightweight body and breathtaking speed.

Thus whilst Mr Turner was being bitten by midges in the enveloping Scotch mist, his backside doubtless sore from the punishment meted out by the rigid framed Terrier, it is tempting to think that he could foresee a more comfortable time when the populace whom he was trying to attract, might one day be drawn to his cars in the way he had witnessed in the States. But that would need a new road system like the one he had seen across the Atlantic and when it came, Mr Turner would be waiting.

In a final twist of fate, Sir William ended up buying Daimler off BSA some years after it had been touched by Mr Turner's magic pencil and included the intellectual property rights to the magnificent Turner V-8s. These were less well known than his XK range particularly after Jaguar's string of Le Mans victories. And as a direct competitor to his own superb engine, Sir William was determined to satisfy a long held curiosity. He took the larger of the Turner V-8s and put it into one of his own Jaguar Mark 10 Limousines that was destined for the American market. At the MIRA test centre it out performed Jaguars finest and the prototype promptly 'disappeared' and the model was never put into production. Sir William developed his XK engine into the Jaguar V-12 that was for many years the fastest production saloon car in the world. But had he been in business with Mr Turner, the more promising Daimler V-8s could have sent automotive history in an altogether different direction. Much water would pass under the very bridge from which Mr Turner allowed himself a moment's contemplation before these events came to pass and for now exports stood between austere Britain and the realisation of the material rewards that America had so quickly achieved.

In 1953, before the coming of that road or even television reception, the Gaffers were starting to feel isolated in a land still shaped more by it's history than a modern populace on the move. They witnessed the shadows on the road, smelt the damp of the undisturbed woodland and felt the cool breeze that occasionally blows down the Killiecrankie Pass but thought little of it.

By 4 pm the Gaffers had conquered Glen Gary and pulled up for another tea break in Dalwhinnie. Thereafter they climbed higher and higher on the seemingly never-ending road. The cairns and glens looked on disdainfully as their silence was briefly disturbed. Occasionally the road dropped onto the low fertile land below the peaks on which crofters eked out a living. They pressed on, resisting the temptation to pay a visit to the Tomatin distillery. Finally Drummossie Muir fell away and they commenced their long drop into the capital of the Pictish Kingdom, Inverness.

Night fell on the Moray Firth and the Terriers put their lights on. They were able to pick out the road signs for the battlefield of Culloden as they sped by. Awaiting their arrival in Station Square was a lone piper chiselled from Purbeck stone with a sphinx at his feet; a memorial to the Cameron Highlanders who fell in Egypt and the Sudan. He survived the ravages of the stray dog school of architecture of the 1960s, but sadly Mr Turner's destination has not. But on the raw evening of Friday the 9th of October, 1953 the thick walls of the old Royal Caledonian Hotel on the banks of the River Ness held back the mist that tumbles down from the river's source where the monster tends to stay put.

MotorCycling magazine went on to record the days performance:-

> *For any sort of machine today's 263 mile trip from Carlisle through Lanark, Stirling, Perth, Kilikrankie and Kinguisse to Inverness would have been tough going, yet the lightweights took to the Highland's hazards with relish.*

Nothing like the relish with which the Gaffers escaped the mist rolling down the river from Loch Ness as they tripped up the marble steps and through the doors of the Royal Caledonian. The fire took the edge off the cold and the golden glow of the columned reception lifted their spirits. Whatever the Highland weather would throw at them tonight would fail to make its presence felt at a dinner table draped in linen and laid with hallmarked silverware. It was to the usual standard. Here Dame Anna Neagle, premier star of films throughout the thirties and forties, had opened the ballroom. Royalty came from all over Europe, frequently swept in by the Daimler cars that Mr Turner had helped to design. The mist closed in as the Gaffers sat around their dinner table. They were reflective now that the end was in sight. From now on the ring of the phone, production targets and the bark of Mr Turner would replace this week of fresh air, food and their boss being in a most agreeable frame of mind. By now Mr Turner was allowing the forthcoming sales battle that he would fight at the Earls Court motorcycle show in a couple of weeks time to invade his thoughts. He did not know the praise the press would heap upon the Terriers until he read these lines the following week:-

Their afternoon appetite for rapid mileage consumption was insatiable, and they treated the Grampians with disdain – to the extent of covering 117 miles in precisely three hours

By midnight the shadows had fallen across the array of weapons that lined the stair wall. The foe they faced lay deep in the mud of the fields of Culloden five miles from where Mr Turner and the Gaffers slept soundly.

HOLLYWOOD STOLE MY JACKET

I rose with the sun the following morning. Unfortunately so did the Scottish Rasta who stood next to me at a sink in the toilet block. We did not speak which would have been particularly difficult for him as he was vigorously cleaning his teeth. His tube of 'toothpaste' read 'sooths itching and reduces piles'. It was a good time to leave.

I eased up at the exit of the site, noting that all was still, and then it dawned on me that this was the old road. I turned north and ambled down a route lined with rock and vegetation at its very edge. It was early morning and the milk had not yet been delivered to the cottages along the way. If Mr Turner should make his presence felt, it would be now, when we were alone on the quiet of some Highland road. That occasional abandoned petrol station may have served him and I tried to imagine three Terriers parked around the rusting petrol pumps. But it was all limited to my imagination, the reality being nothing more than the wind shuddering a long locked door.

The Thunderbird took the climbs with ease where Mr Turner had had to strain his tiny Terrier. We took the Killiecrankie Pass and dropped onto the old stone bridge. It was 6.45 am on Friday the 26th of June some fifty-four years since Mr Turner had passed this way. Many a generation of salmon had passed to and fro since he gazed into these waters. I had stopped for a photo shoot but chose to linger in case I heard the rumbling of three Terriers carried on the wind. I strained but all I heard was the mewing of the buzzard above the running water and so decided to leave.

This was the old road I remembered so well; one that bore witness to every change in the landscape. Behind the woodland and over the hill the new A9 would shortly grind into its domineering existence as the world shot through without a thought. But for now it was 1953 and every bit as quiet. Indeed, Mr Turner could ride into view at any minute.

Through an opening in the trees I spied the magnificent Blair Athol castle, home of the Athol Highlanders, Europe's only legal private army. The army are responsible for the defence of the castle, estate and the locals. Should you ever have the misfortune to spill the pint of someone wearing the tartan of Clan Murray of Athol, buy them another because they may have lots of mates with swords.

I rode on but Mr Turner was toying with me now, or perhaps it was the Department of Transport. The old road had to continue without me. It was closed for all but cyclists and I was forced to rub shoulders with convoys of European trucks on the new road as it tantalizingly swept away from Mr Turner's route that was now punctuated by patches of grass growing in its centre.

The English had turned positively feeble over the weather during the last week, but to the Highlanders it was something they took in their stride. It rains a lot here and the mountains are shrouded in mist the rest of the time anyway.

The road wound on, ever higher, having taken the sudden climbs out of the mountainside. Now it was lined with perpendicular aluminium poles to mark the way when the snowdrifts cover the road.

I left the tree line behind and the rain slammed into the moor. I could see the weather forming down the valley and gathering speed before dumping on me and then passing. Convoys eased passed me as I pulled into a parking place. Civil engineers had braced the mountainside with metal cables to prevent landslides and beyond these and down in the valley ran the lonely thread of the old road meandering through fields of sheep and thistles. Occasionally it passed isolated cottages whose tracks ran down to its edge. For these people life is now much quieter. I strained from the high ground, peering into the valley below. I could swear I had seen a solitary motorcyclist ease up at one of the crofts. I waited for the rider to re-emerge whilst the passing trucks buffeted me from behind. It was like a tap on the shoulder as fate whispered in my ear, "stop trying, you wouldn't like 1953".

Finally I found a sign for the Highland visitor centre and on following it found myself briefly on that old road once more. The centre was modern and like a control tower with the panoramic café on the top floor. Here an Italian wrapped in a cashmere coat drank frothy coffee and timid tourists looked out at a wild scene. "I told you we should have stayed at home", said one wife to her shell-shocked husband.

Broadsheets piled up on comfortable chairs, and here you could recharge your phone, digital camera or gain internet access.

"Yooze the Treeumph ootsade aye?" said a bearded giant to the only bloke in the café in motorcycle gear. I was still in Clan Murray country so smart Alec quips were not the order of the day.

"Ave a bake ma self, sooze ma waif".

He stood nervously beside me with his hands thrust down in his pockets whilst his eyes darted around the room. A proper Highlander drawn down from the mountain and ill at ease in a 'crowded' café with six windswept customers. Finally my toasted Italian pannini with mozerella and sun dried tomatoes arrived which caught his disgusted glance.

"Ya birty woofta" I expected, but instead enjoyed his parting good wishes with "watch the roodz and enjoy yaself".

I stepped out of the café and then paused for a moment's reflection. It was silent but for the gently dripping foliage. I sat on the dry stone wall and looked up and down the empty road. If Mr Turner decided to reappear at this point he would be hard pressed to find any changes. I waited in the brief stillness until it dawned on me that I was not entirely sure that I actually wanted to meet Mr Turner. Bosses from the fifties bordered on the divine and you knew not to speak unless you were spoken to. His world was not mine and I feared that I had been allowing the past to overshadow the present; something that is easy when one age exists only in the imagination with its frailties sifted out. Even so some comments still echoed down the ages:-

Edward Turner was an exceptional, if irascible individual. His contributions to motorcycling dictated design trends for three or four decades, and the ricochets of that influence are still being felt today.

These words came from a 1979 copy of *Classic Bike* magazine. As I looked at the rain settling on my own Triumph nearly three decades later I had to conclude that they are still true.

But what of Mr Turner himself? Would the great man speak to me when we met, as I was sure we would before my ride was complete. I remembered that Mr Turner 'could be by turns tyrannical, charming and inspirational'.

The road was riddled with puddles, always a threat to a Terrier with its spindly tyres, but Mr Turner was a former racer and I expected him to be contemptuous of the easy ride that I by contrast enjoyed courtesy of modern wide tyres.

The rain briefly eased and was replaced by a gentle wind that shook the water off the leaves.

I consoled myself with the thought that for every person who intensely disliked Mr Turner, there was another who was equally devoted to him, which was perhaps merely a reflection of his many sides. On any day in the office he could throw things at staff one moment, only to ask if they had enjoyed the weekend's motorcycle racing the next. Those who had witnessed him falling off a motorcycle one afternoon may have spent the evening praying that he had not noticed their smirk, only to find him thanking them for their concern the following morning. But as the selling season approached his temper was always that bit shorter than usual and in particular in the run up to the Earls Court show. Often he could be found at his drawing desk beneath his sunburst clock that remained in his office until the day of the factory's demolition. On one such occasion he sent a brief message to his secretary, "Send for Davies". Ivor Davies blasphemed and thought "What does he want now?" With that he nervously picked up every conceivable scrap of paper, confident of one thing, "If you hadn't got the right one you were in trouble". Many times Mr Turner had given him a job in the morning, only to chase him by 4 pm on the dot to see if it had been done. On this particular morning Ivor had been told to do 'a proper Triumph job' in designing the stand for the show. As everyone knew at Meriden, there are three ways to do a job; 'the right way, the wrong way and the Triumph way'. On this occasion Mr Turner started talking without even looking up, "Well, Davies, let's have a look at those designs for the show stand". He turned from his drawing board and wheeled his chair up to his desk. Ivor placed the papers before him and spread them out. Mr Turner slowly shook his head as he looked at each in turn. Ivor felt his designs were good but clearly not good enough; consequently he braced himself. "Come on, let's go into the drawing office", came the mild but firm response. Mr Turner reached for his pencil. "Right, two columns Davies. One at each end of the stand". Even if Mr Turner was not really related to JMW Turner, a pencil in his hand could be directed to create a work of art with ease.

"Now round the top we'll have four chrome strips with our logo in the middle. Tube lights Davies, I want tube lights behind each strip so the whole thing is flood lit and the name stands out"

He handed Ivor his drawing.

"I want there to be no doubt precisely where Triumph are. It'll be like moths to a bright light. Have it ready by the morning Davies. And goodnight to you."

And with that the office door slammed shut. Ivor looked at Mr Turner's design. It was an impressive result of a typical burst of energy that did indeed go on to dominate the Earls Court show for many years.

So he was an artist. And talent is often allowed to excuse unpleasant personality traits. And it is well recorded that news that he would be visiting the experimental department to test ride a bike would 'create an effect that was like an electric charge jolting the department'. But his most famous habit was displayed following one of his breakneck rides when:-

If Turner was dissatisfied with the machine and there was no one waiting to take the bike from his hands on his return to the factory, it was not unknown for him to simply step off the motorcycle, wantonly allowing it to crash to the ground.

The rain had returned but Mr Turner had not. I smiled to myself as I pressed the starter on my modern Triumph and it roared into life. There would be no dropping this Triumph to the ground for want of satisfaction.

The old road was short and deposited me once again on the new road where I was engulfed in lorry spray. Even so, every mile was a photo opportunity as my records bear witness. The peaks of distant mountains were dramatic against the wild sky, Carn Phris Mhóir, Beinn Bhreac Mhór and Carn na Saobhaidh, as majestic as they are difficult to pronounce. They looked angry in the rain and smiled in the sun that suddenly came out between weather fronts. Ordinarily my mood would change with the weather too, as unease would be ushered out by euphoria. But for today it was euphoria all the way. For Mr Turner, this may have been the point at which he finally thought that his Terriers had bitten off more than they could chew. However I marvelled at my bike as it burbled contentedly through the Highland's hardest.

My ride was of course an easy one; no Ted Simon adventure this. Yet I still harboured a fear of finding myself with a flat tyre, at night and in the rain. Consequently I planned for everything on the basis that if it could go wrong it would. In the course of my preparation I came across a salesman who sold Triumphs from a showroom that looked like a hairdresser's salon. Terry was my best friend when he thought he could sell me a new bike. When all I wanted was two ten millimetre bolts the smile dropped from his face and came to rest about his slip-ons. We were destined not to get on if for no other reason than his choice of footwear. Tony, the ageing Rocker from Bolney, who runs the Motorcycle Workshop, knew exactly where his 10mm bolts were. That's useful because they hold the back wheel in place. Little tip; if he has not got grease under his finger nails do not trust him. In fact do not trust anyone in motorcycling without heritage. You want engineers looking after you when you top the ton, not accountants. I actually chose my sponsors and not the other way around. So Scottoiler kept me lubricated, OKO kept me inflated, Avon kept me upright and Tony the Rocker brought them all together. But it was Bob Heath who literally showed me the way. A former tester at BSA, he took their 500cc B50 over the line to clinch first place in the Shell Sport 500 championship in 1971. Now a guy who will do that himself is the man I want making my visor and it was a revelation. No matter how bad the weather, my vision was perfect. I recalled the wisdom of youth in an extract from Hooligan Films:-

> Someone will stick their head in a helmet made by someone in China who has never seen a motorcycle. That strikes me as absurd.

I fastened the collar on my jacket, put away my camera and braced myself for another wave of the Highland's toughest.

My jacket alas, caused me difficulty. I had read the bike magazines from the fifties when everything was made in Britain. Barbour and Belstaff emerged as the expensive but everlasting classic motorcycle jacket. The latter seemed the one to approach for sponsorship as the Winter family matriarch, my Aunty Joyce, used to work in the factory in Stoke-on-Trent. But now, nobody seemed to know where Belstaff were; they existed in the ether of the internet as a brand, and a very British brand at that, but finding them was impossible. They seemed to have been there as long as motorcycling, making the jacket before the throw away society. They were noticeably more durable and sported a tourist's tartan on the inside. I was sure I could help them sell truck loads and finally I tracked down a mirror-lined boutique in West London and duly gave them a call. An indifferent receptionist answered and claimed never to have heard of Aunty Joyce. In the background I could hear unpacking, the hallmark of imports. This garment that blazes the Union Jack is made abroad. And they do not answer my emails, which is perhaps less surprising. The image of the Belstaff is what it is because of the lads at the Ace Café and elsewhere but now the 'brand' appears in Hollywood blockbusters. Apparently their jackets are worn by 'the stars' and when I considered buying one they came in at about £160, which is about right. The Hollywood effect sent them up to £500, which most certainly is not. Of course I could have helped them 'strengthen the brand', but perhaps not quite as much as the King of Cool: Steve McQueen. He loved and indeed lived in his and wore it whilst riding in the American team on a Triumph in the International Six Day Trial. Belstaff tried to make the most of that, attracting the headline, 'Ripping Off The King Of Cool Just Isn't Cool'. Steve's son Chad launched a lawsuit against Belstaff accusing them of jeopardising the goodwill and value of the McQueen trademark. They would have had a lot less trouble from me and Aunty Joyce.

The sun came out and the old road reappeared by way of another token gesture and took on the title of 'heritage route'. I took it passing over bridges spanning wide rivers before riding down high streets fronted by local businesses and then headed out of the north exit to continue my journey. At one point I crested the brow of a hill where the meandering old road ran briefly right next to the new one. It passed two rock outcrops either side of the road, both like polished pewter with the sun on their drenched surface. Here the old traveller could marvel at the hand of God as he viewed the road winding down the mountain. On the new road the outcrop had been blasted away and the modern travellers' thoughts are drawn to avoiding being flattened by trucks full of frozen prawns.

The road filled with caravans and lorries as the countryside opened out along the Moray Firth. Beyond the estuary was another range of mountains that was the final leg to the far north. It was my uncertainty about the time this would take that is responsible for my passing the sign for the battlefield of Culloden without stopping.

Mr Turner did not go through petrol at anything like the rate that I did as he passed these sacred grounds. Consequently I was relieved to cross the River Ness and pull up in a petrol station. Further up the river is the new Royal Caledonian Hotel, on the site of the old. Dame Anna Neagle no longer graces its fine ballroom as it has long gone and been replaced by a building from the stray dog school of architecture. Now it is part of a giant chain and had reps leaning against its prefabricated walls between 'conferences' enjoying a fag when I passed. There are no awards for architecture to be dished out here, just a letter to some distant head office from the local authority, ticking them off for the state of their kitchens. Having felt that I was briefly getting closer to the spirit of Mr Turner, I knew he would not linger here and neither did I.

THE CALL OF THE SEA

The Gaffers pulled out of the Royal Caledonian Hotel at precisely 7 am on Saturday the 10th of October, 1953. It was the final day and not without incident as *MotorCycling* magazine reported:-

> *Rounding a typically Scottish never ending curve, Bob Fearon ran out of road. Rather than drop the model and possibly bend it, he clung on like grim death as he took to the grass verge and executed a simply terrific leap when the machine hit a concealed culvert.*

Those 'never ending curves' had not yet been ironed out by the coming of 'the road' and Mr Turner was forced down the Beauly Firth, over Black Isle and round Cromarty Firth. He may have had only 158 miles ahead of him but they were very different from mine.

Now he was out ahead and on his own. The final hours of the Gaffers' Gallop were thoughtful ones, for the end of their week on the road was imminent. Mr Turner followed the line of the estuary before crossing at Bonar Bridge only to retrace his steps on the opposite bank. Now the road took him out along the coast and passed Dunrobin Castle. He could see the vast openness of the North Sea until it gave way to the curvature of the earth. Mr Turner had never lost his love of the sea and had a succession of yachts on the South Coast. He had also started his working life as a junior telegraphy officer on the armed merchantman, the *SS Hindustan*, and on the evening of the 31st of January, 1953 his maritime instinct had been aroused by the weather reports. He knew that nature was putting together what mariners know as that rare phenomena; the perfect storm.

Britain was still a maritime nation and many families had someone at sea. High tides, a depression and driving winds combined to cause the sea to surge down the coast of Britain. The vessel *Princess Victoria* went down off Belfast with the loss of 133 lives. The Lincolnshire coast faced waves six metres high, whereas the vessels at sea faced waves the height of skyscrapers and when they broke overhead there was such a weight of water above them that they could not float and were lost for good.

Mr Turner travelled up a coast totally dependent on fishing and still bearing the scars of the flood. The sea was everything and the thousands of tiny vessels their livelihood. There was no room for romance here; it was survival amongst those who dared go out in the heaviest storms. Hard men of questionable sanity lived on this bleak coast where it is dark for months at a time. Superstition was their logic and they feared the ships bell tolling of its own accord or a bird tapping at the wheelhouse window. And on that fateful night the Highland community had its sons at sea. Word quickly spread that the 7,000 ton vessel, the *Clan Macquarrie* had run aground. The Life Saving Auxiliary Company had an 18 mile overland trip from Stornoway. They then dragged their life saving gear over a cart track and then open ground. Rocket line after rocket line was fired and failed to reach the stricken vessel. Mr Turner heard reports of the unfolding drama:-

> They (the LSA team) were soaked to the skin and several men were blown into ditches which had become raging torrents, their hands were swollen and puffy with cold, legs numb to the knees, and faces caked with mud, oil and salt.

By daybreak they had achieved the largest ship to shore rescue in history with all 66 crew and the vessel's cat safely distributed amongst Highland cottages and sat beside their roaring fires.

Mr Turner's route was lined with reminders that not all the struggles of that dark night had ended so happily. The tide still brought in the flotsam's silent testimony and the boatyards were littered with the skeletal remains of vessels. This was still the era of the 'stiff upper lip', but Mr Turner knew that look in the eye when he saw it.

Mr Turner rode on passed the Ord of Caithness, allowing his thoughts to wander. The road wound on seemingly forever and petrol stations were few but at over 100 mpg that was of little concern to Mr Turner.

They passed between the Loch of Yarrows and the fishing village of Sarclet before dropping into the last major town of Wick. The winds of change were just starting to blow even in 1953 and the town had performed its last Herring Queen ceremony. From now on the area would be more famous for the Dounreay nuclear research establishment than fishing.

The three Terriers lined up north of Wick adjacent to Castle Gringoe. The road ahead ran adjacent to the sweeping sandy Sinclair Bay. They were ready for the last few miles.

SUNSHINE GALORE

Few people benefited more from the new road than I and the Moray Firth was an easy journey over a modern bridge, as indeed was the Cromarty Firth. I was on my own over these vast waters and enjoying a peculiar sense of tranquillity. I too was nearly there, but where was Mr Turner? As I crossed the Dornoch Firth I suspected that he was at Bonar Bridge and I was sure that he would catch me when I made one of my many stops for petrol.

The conclusion that Inverness was nearly the end of my journey was the wrong one as even with the aid of the bridges, the road seemed never ending. I occasionally thought I caught the scent of vintage motor oil in the air, but perhaps this was just my overactive imagination.

Where Mr Turner had enjoyed fine weather until Inverness, it was only when I left this Highland capital that the weather actually improved. I passed Dunrobin Castle but unlike Mr Turner my thoughts were not with the sea but the land. These Highlands had clearly been well populated once. I noted increasing numbers of derelict stone cottages scattered across the hillside. I had always known about the Highland Clearances but despite my knowledge of Scotland I was shocked by the extent. The cottages stand like tombstones and occasionally people live in static caravans alongside them, but I noticed that none seemed to have been re-inhabited.

At the turn of the 19th century, landowners felt they could get more from their land if they replaced the people with sheep. Like Culloden, the plans to clear crofts were carried out by Scottish aristocrats on their own. But it was an Englishman, the Duke of Sutherland who is loathed beyond compare. He was appalled at the conditions of his tenants and decided that farming could not support their lifestyle, although their very existence proved otherwise. Around 1810, the tenants were burned out and the sheep moved in. He then shoved thousands of families out to the coast where they should magically transform themselves from farmers to fishermen. Or leave for America, taking their long memories with them.

His Grace, the Duke, thought this was trendy social reform and was motivated by 'high principles' but was let down by their implementation. At this point even the most measured and sensitive commentator gives in to the temptation that expletives present. His Grace has a massive statue on a 76ft pedestal that is covered in bird shit and graffiti. That it still stands at all is a towering monument to the tolerance of the Scots and little else.

I now passed the Ord of Caithness under bright sunshine and found it impossible not to throttle back because the road was just too good. Down the straights I let her have it before winding up the empty ribbon of open road between the mountainside, and open sea. The road started climbing again and the gates sporting the sign; 'Road Closed – Snow' were wide open so up and through I flew. Naughty, I know. And then I went on to reserve petrol.

Villages baked in the sun on the distant headland, but the petrol stations were few. Should I gamble and turn inland? I risked it and came across three road workers loading their tools into a van. I turned the bike around and they glared at me. I switched off the engine and took off my helmet.

"Excuse me, could you tell me where the nearest petrol station is?"

They looked back quizzically.

"Look", said one of them pointing at my petrol tank.

"Treeumph"

"Aye rate, it is that."

"Dya knoo, thays a fella from the Treeumph factory raiding his bake tay John O'Groats ta dee."

"Really, I wonder why they didn't tell me?"

"Aye, 'twas in the Journal."

And then I remembered that I had spoken to the *John O'Groats Journal*.

"Oh, that's me."

"Fo' charity, aye?"

"Yes that's right."

We chatted and I decided it was time for a photo opportunity. All three stood in front of their van with my bike in the foreground. Arty, you can imagine, I am sure.

"Hey!" exclaimed one of them, holding out his hand to stop me. He swirled round, closing the sliding door of his van to reveal the logo, which he slapped with pride: "Scottish Water."

"Aah petrol, tek the rood, keep goin' but didnae worry 'cause we'll be behind ya"

And with that I was off, albeit gently until I came across my final petrol station at Thrumster in Caithness. When I came out of the station the white van was parked in the forecourt with the window down.

"Commee heeya and tek this" as an arm stretched out of the window and passed me a generous donation without mentioning if they had seen a rider on a Triumph Terrier.

Moments later I was on my own once more and silence returned. I looked up and down the road. In all my time on this journey I had but a few moments when my day would be indistinguishable from Mr Turners. This was one such and I felt almost chillingly close to meeting the man whose reputation came storming down the decades. Of course I was pensive, but there was another side to Mr Turner that came to the fore in the easy going American atmosphere of his Bahaman home to which he initially retired.

Mr Turner moved freely and easily between the island's luxury homes in which partygoers of all ages and from all walks of life mixed comfortably, something which he found very agreeable. When the party was over he would often retire to his own home to practice his fine baritone voice that, to his regret, had been neglected since his youth, when his chosen career ensured the art's loss became motorcycling's gain.

During the day he would while away the hours having taken up the hobby of radio ham thus harking back to his days in the Merchant Navy. He seemed to have little trouble making friends the world over or amongst his neighbours.

In short, all was well but Mr Turner felt his family's interests would be better served if he returned to England. This did not happen before he had established a reputation with the local GP who was aware of his diabetes. One aspect of the lifestyle that did not suit him was the abundance of American food. The GP just could not persuade him that ice cream was not good for him and Mr Turner responded with the truly unique argument that it did not contain any sugar. Sometimes it was just best to smile benevolently and shake your head. I too found myself doing just that as I glanced up and down the still empty road before setting off once more.

I passed through Wick and eased up alongside Castle Gringoe. Ahead of me was the sweeping Sinclair Bay. With a tank full of petrol and 900cc beneath me, that would be a good bend to take: here goes! My rev counter briefly hit the red line then I dropped the clutch. I was sure to catch up with Mr Turner now.

THE FIGHTING TEMERAIRE

I leant the bike over at a jaunty angle as I swept along Sinclair Bay. In my imagination Mr Turner had done the same thing on his single cylinder Terrier as it bounced in and out of the ruts where the Thunderbird surged with ease, its giant back wheel smoothing out the road. Where Mr Turner would have clenched the bar with his chin on the tank as the Terrier strained, I sat upright with one hand on the throttle able to twist it to twice the speed of the Terrier.

Like Mr Turner, I was reflective because my week on the road was coming to an end too. I slowed up reverentially as I passed Noss Head and Freswick Bay. We were nearly there. The road to John O'Groats is long and windswept. On still mornings all that can be heard is the call of the curlew as it makes its way across the barren expanse.

Mr Turner rode towards John O'Groats, easing off the throttle as he coasted towards the hotel on the shore. His purpose was to demonstrate that his Terrier could meet the needs of a nation that had to make a little go far. The single cylinder wonder was in keeping with the rhythms of nature, its power within comprehension, its form the product of Mr Turner's flowing pencil but most important of all, it was cheap. Like all of Mr Turner's designs, it obeyed the laws of nature so its clean lines cut through the air rather than trying to barge it open. The following week *MotorCycling* magazine would inform a thrifty nation:-

> *The observed 1,008 miles had been covered in a total running time 27 hours and 29 minutes giving an overall average speed of 38.85 mph with an average fuel consumption of 108.8 mpg - quite a bit better than the 30 mph and 100 mpg which formed the target when the team left for Land's End.*

I rumbled towards the John O'Groats Hotel with the ever present worry of finding a petrol station before I ran dry. With regard to my petrol consumption, I only knew that I had spent considerably more than Mr Turner.

The ghostly structure of the John O'Groats Hotel came into view. In the reception a lone figure gazes into the car park. He has spent many solitary hours admiring his favourite painting, *The Fighting Temeraire*, by his namesake JMW Turner. He knows that progress dictates that anything one creates will ultimately be 'tugged to her berth to be broken up'. He knew that it would happen one day to his Terrier and the Tiger Cub it evolved into. But would the end be as undignified as that of the ghostly *Temeraire* as she is pulled along a still Thames, her form in keeping with the laws of nature to cut through the water at the whim of the wind, now servient to a blackened tug boat scurrying along like a water beetle?

Somebody once wrote that 'it is better to travel than arrive' and on closer inspection of the John O'Groats Hotel, I was inclined to agree. I eased up at the entrance of the car park and gazed around. When Mr Turner arrived here fifty-four years earlier, the future of his single cylinder wonder hung in the balance. Would it meet the demands of a very different age? A week after the conclusion of the 1953 Gaffer's Gallop, Mr Turner was gearing up for the Earls Court Motorcycle Show.

The 'First Show Issue' of *MotorCycling* hit Mr Turner's desk a fortnight after the Gaffers' Gallop. The editor, Graham Walker (Murray's Dad) declared to a deferential readership that:-

> *It is particularly fitting that Her Majesty's Foreign Minister, the Rt Hon Anthony Eden, PC, MC should open the show.*

This issue was a weighty tome that amounted to a mutual congratulation of the efforts of a nation recently engaged in mortal struggle and now locked in economic battle. But Britain was still a militarised state and in a militarised state of mind as Walker continued:-

Such is the efficiency with which the ...Motorcycle Manufacturers Traders Union stage their shows that an exhibitor who failed to meet the deadline would feel like HM Bateman's Guardsman who dropped his rifle on parade.

This was of little interest to Mr Turner as he pensively flicked through the pages. However he would have whole-heartedly agreed with the editorial, which read:-

The British motorcycle industry has played a very worthy part in the battle for overseas business upon the outcome of which our economic stability so largely depends.

All together now... Meanwhile the demobbed ranks were free of the worries of leadership and busied themselves with the magazine's report on the Cheltenham Home Guard Motorcycle Club trial where Dad's Army had applied their substantial organisational skills to amateur motor sport. It was an orderly time in which one was still defined by one's regiment or cricket club. Or, in Mr Turner's case, sales figures. Finally, just before Avon Tyres' double page advert wherein Geoff Duke disclosed 'the secret of how leading riders have helped develop this wonderful new tyre for you', Mr Turner spotted something. He flicked back through the pages until his eyes fell upon an exploded diagram above a footnote that read:-

Making its first public appearance next week, the Triumph Tiger Cub.

While Mr Turner worried about every detail, the punters enjoyed a parallel world in which they took advantage of their increasing mobility. 'Up In Town For The Show?' ran the next article in which collared and tied bikers (or motorcyclists as they were then known) were encouraged to dine at The Trocadero on Shaftsbury Avenue or to go to view *The Conquest Of Everest* at the Warner Theatre in Leicester Square. No mention was made of the cafés springing up around the Elephant and Castle where quiffed youths were no longer deferential.

Finally two pages after the floor plan of Earls Court in the middle of the magazine, Mr Turner found the full page advert he had been looking for:-

Triumph presents the 200cc Tiger Cub

By the addition of a mere 50cc the Terriers of the Gaffers' Gallop had grown into a Tiger Cub. It was never destined to be a legend, but the means by which one could move seamlessly from a Cub to a fully grown Tiger 650 or even a Bonnie for the really hairy chested. It was all there from the nacelle to the mouth organ tank badge. Once they were on a Cub, they were on a Triumph for life. Mr Turner had got it absolutely right.

Sales soared and in one year 13,000 models rolled off the production line. Laughable figures in today's disposable recyclable age, but very different in an era where the motorcycle was built for life. Generations of teenagers learned on them, loved on them and grew up on them. It was the small bike with big bike feel and big boys' performance. In those days fun was cheap, easy to mend and you could ride it without being a carbon Big Foot. The Terrier/Cub counted amongst its satisfied customers, His Majesty the King of Nepal and Baudouin, King of The Belgians. Over an eighteen year production period the bikes were exported to 153 countries ranging from Angola and Nicaragua to France and America. In total Mr Turner's 'little factory in England' produced 112,672 models of the very bike that he arrived on at John O'Groats on Saturday the 10th of October, 1953. By 1968 it had served its purpose in an age where austerity was forgotten and a new generation was tired of hearing its virtue. The French army took their final delivery and the very last batch were made from spares and delivered to Slocombes of Neasden, London on the 18th of June, 1970. The world had moved on.

But in 1953, Mr Turner knew nothing of the above success; only that one day the Terrier/Cub would have had its day like the *Fighting Temeraire*. He wondered how many of his styling cues that were the spirit of his motorcycle, making it more than a mere mass of nuts and bolts, would survive. By contrast the *Temeraire* was pulled into Beatson's shipyard at Rotherhithe. Its heart of solid oak would never feature in ship design again. It was replaced by a vessel that bore no resemblance to its gracious predecessor and was described by William Thackeray rather satanically as:-

> The little demon of a steamer is belching out a volume of foul, lurid, red-hot, malignant smoke, paddling furiously.

I rode into the car park at walking pace. Occasionally the engine snatched at the chain. There was no hiding the fact that this was a thoroughly modern motorcycle trying to look old. Triumph were very cautious about making a 'real' Triumph having established themselves as makers of thoroughly modern muscle bikes. It was not easy turning a top-heavy 900cc superbike into a 1950s 'sit up 'n' beg', but it was worth it. In 1995 the influential weekly *Motor Cycle News* greeted Triumph's foray into Mr Turner's design studio with the front page headline that read 'Triumph's Brilliant New 900

Raises The Stakes In The Retro Race'. The bike was tipped to become the star of the forthcoming Alexandra Palace Show and there in the middle pages, under the headline 'The Badge Of Success', was a photograph of the iconic mouth organ tank badge, straight from the 1950s. The bike outsold all other Triumph models and ushered in the decision to bring back the Bonnie.

I turned around in the car park, switched off the engine and took off my helmet. I looked over my shoulder but there was no apparition that I could see, to give me an approving nod, not least as the windows were whitewashed. I sat there for a moment recalling the Terrier from the National Motorcycle Museum and how small it would be if measured up alongside me now.

> *Now the sunset's breezes shiver,*
> *And she's fading down the river,*
> *And in England's song forever,*
> *She's the Fighting Temeraire"*

Nice one!

'And then the wind blew the tripod over...' Was Mr Turner in a bad mood or having a laugh?

Two Years Later

When the reserve tank ran dry too, and the engine choked and died… I let the bike roll off the asphalt onto the grass under the shade of a tree…and stood by the bike looking up and down the country road and across the field of green wheat wondering who was going to help me this time, and what it would lead to. I did not doubt that help would come and with it most probably some unexpected twist in my fortunes. It had taken years to achieve that measure of confidence and calm, and as I waited I allowed myself some pleasure in knowing it.

Classic lines from *Jupiter's Travels*, but when it happened to me in the early hours of the morning I was less sanguine. It was 2 am when my bike came to a standstill in darkest rural Surrey just six miles from my home. I sat on a conveniently placed park bench alongside the cricket pitch and gazed at the stars.

Despite my current predicament I was on a 'high' having enjoyed the day we were never supposed to see, the Triumph Bonneville's 50th birthday: an anniversary that was about so much more than a mere motorbike.

I had left at 4 am the previous day, tripping over my son's wooden 'rocking motorbike', waking him in the process. Now he had the capacity to actually say, "Daddy don't go", but instead asked for a drink, thus waking his Mum. Moments later I spared the entire neighbourhood the same fate when I gently coasted the bike down the road and set off for Warwickshire. I crested hills and cut through the mist that lay in the hollows as the sun rose, or at least that's how it romantically appeared from the saddle of my Triumph.

I arrived at the British Motor Heritage Centre as hundreds of Triumphs rolled by under the early morning sun. Hairy bikers and the distinctly well dressed were mixing with ease, blissfully unaware of what Triumph's rivals used to say about the prospects of meeting 'nicer people' elsewhere. I was now about to see in the flesh, the very people who made this story.

After years of reading about Mr Turner's family I would shortly set eyes upon them. I tried to imagine how two small girls who I had seen in a photograph from the late fifties would appear today. I was reflective whilst waiting for their younger brother to open the celebration. I was, by putting faces to the characters in my book, drawing my own odyssey to a close and it was about time. My own son was growing up during my indulgence and he had inevitably changed everything. But for now I looked at the people at the foot of the stage and realised that time was passing for all of us. I had spent the last two years suspended, sometimes sentimentally, in the post war years as if the millennium had been an inadequate substitute. I had to come to terms with the fact that the people who had shaped events then, would now be very mature, shall we say. I cast my eye across the gathering crowd as a chap about my own age gave a speech. Of course, Edward Turner junior was born a couple of years before me, Mr Turner having started his family relatively late in life.

People that seemed strangely familiar, shook hands, shared reminisces, in some cases having crossed continents to see each other. Clearly they had shared something very special.

The crowd slowly dispersed when Edward pronounced the celebration open. I looked across these ageing faces that had once made the newsreels in the seventies and eighties and then back at the Turner family. These were the girls who went exploring their father's stately pile at Abbotsville, listened to his stories on tape while he was away on business and to whom their dress sizes were known off by heart. At the front was Charmian who visited her father's factory one last time before a demolition ball swung into it removing perhaps the last vestige of a life of toil and sweeping away the dreams of a workers' co-operative. I held back from introducing myself for fear that meeting someone out of my book in the flesh might somehow break the spell. Just then an elderly gentleman next to me rose to his feet. The face from the documentaries, now a little frailer but still very alert, the works manager Mr John Nelson. I watched him for some time, cautious about invading his privacy, but it was clear he possessed an amenable temperament. Excusing myself I added, "hello, Mr Nelson, you don't know me but I'm…"

He looked at me as he took my hand, "Oh thank goodness for that, it always worries me when I can't recall names."

He was engaging; "Yes, I worked very closely with ET."

People milled about him as he added somewhat wistfully, "It was a very happy place to work". I mentioned this book, "Oh you'll be wanting some photographs next. I've thousands. They are all out of order because during the sit-in nobody appreciated the importance of them so they just threw them around". I commented that today must be quite a special day, to which he looked passed me, thinking for a moment and then laughing, "Yes, well I've told them, once I've seen this day through I can go off and die".

White clouds drifted over us occasionally breaking the brilliant sunshine that set the chrome alight. Not only were the faces of the Workers' Co-operative familiar, so were some of the faces in the crowd. I have spent much of my adult life at these events and if my youth has been misspent then so be it, but the Triumph motorcycle has been alongside me throughout. It was pleasing to see how Triumph riders have not changed over the years even if some had put their 'glad rags' on for the day. Indeed a modern ad agency might be tempted to suggest that, 'you still meet nicer people on a Honda'. To confirm this one Triumph sported the message 'touch my bike, feel my boot'. But the passing years seem to have made Triumph's 'bad boy' image one to be commercially exploited rather than suppressed.

One character strolling towards me needed no introduction. Once schoolboys put posters of him on their bedroom walls as he rounded the racing circuits on the unbeatable Tridents. Percy Tait caught my eye and did not hesitate to speak. A legendary wit, he advised me with a grin "I've had my leg over everyone of 'em", to which I assume he was talking about the assembled motorcycles, but could not be sure.

In the Heritage Centre, on a plinth, was Stormy Mangham's Streamliner along with a display of Triumphs through the ages. Everyone has their own personal favourites and bikers can have some very strong opinions. Anything connected with the sixties seems to attract the highest prices, however my interest in Triumphs coincided with the formation of the Workers' Co-operative. Their products were better finished; more solid and just felt 'real' compared to the motorcycles ridden by those 'nicer people'. In a disposable age, Triumphs looked and, today, proved that they were built to last. These were the old world values that those of my generation, unimpressed with the throw away culture, had the chance to savour, thanks to the Co-operative. In a world of consumer credit and fast filling land-fill sites, the hand crafted Triumph was a timely reminder that it did not have to be this way.

In his book *Unmitigated England*, Peter Ashley writes that one of the pleasures of aesthetics in the past was its subconscious impact, which was:-

One we didn't appreciate until we were either robbed of it or it simply disappeared. Its just that much of what we saw in our everyday lives actually looked rather good, and there was a definite sense of things also looking very different to each other, rather than all the same.

The Co-op's formation also coincided with the publication of one of the most influential books of the twentieth century, EF Schumacher's *Small Is Beautiful, A Study In Economics As If People Mattered*. It introduced 'globalism' and the 'environment' into the economic debate. Sometimes the answers to these problems have been staring you right in the face all along.

The Co-op's struggles became the stuff of documentaries, which even as a child I watched avidly, annoyed as the pundits wrote them off, year in year out. I recall the figure of a young welder and sincere socialist who gave uncomfortable interviews whilst the workers tenaciously faced one crisis after another so that people like me had a choice. That man was John Rosamund, the Chairman of the Workers' Board of Directors. Today I spied John from a distance appearing ill at ease in his Sunday best and still not wishing to attract attention to himself. He had fallen out of the public eye when Meriden closed and kept a deafening silence for decades. I sensed, rightly or wrongly, that the loss of Meriden and the dream of a workers' co-operative still hurt. We shook hands as I told him it was a real pleasure to meet him. Gushing I added, "What you guys did was just fantastic". We chatted and John told me that his own book had taken him two years to write. It covered the period of my childhood and adolescence when I knew that one day I would own a thundering Triumph rather than a 'crotch rocket' because of the defiance of people like John and the rest of the workers.

"I've shed a few tears writing this," he added as I could see he was welling up. John's publisher set up the stand and people started to realise who he was. I retired to let him sign autographs and be photographed shaking their hands. I had not intended to do this myself as I guessed that being a celebrity was the last thing he wanted, but if they were, I was. I placed my hand on his shoulder as we posed for a photograph, "You know John, none of us would be here today if it weren't for you". He either thought I understood what the Co-operative was all about or I was a sentimental prick. Either way I will not forget his parting words, "We certainly tried. We did what we thought was right".

It was the perfect summer's day with bikes and riders baking in the sun's rays with frequent relief being provided by the ranks of cumulus nimbus. The green fields of Middle England never looked so fine as I strolled around soaking up the atmosphere, something I've done a lot of at such events over the years. I met two of my best mates through Triumphs, although when I look at them I sometimes think I deserved to do rather better. One of them was waiting for me beside the police tent, which was the last place I expected to find him. We strolled over to the dapper figure of Norman Hyde, the fastest man on earth (in a sidecar at least). Spying the cover of my copy of John Rosamund's book he announced,

"That's Dobbin!"

An old friend, better known as Bob Haines, was trying to look serious as he stood beside a Bonneville for a photo shoot outside the Meriden factory.

"He swore he could get out of any knot like Houdini, so we took him down to the basement, tied him up and strung him upside down".

Musing for a moment Norman added, "I don't know what health and safety would make of that. People were asking for him all afternoon so I inevitably quipped, 'Oh he's just tied up at the moment'".

I tried to level this with EF Schumacher's view that blessed were those employed in "...work properly conducted in conditions of human dignity and freedom..." The image of the perpetually wriggling Dobbin did not measure up to most people's idea of 'human dignity', but then I suspect *Small Is Beautiful* is read more in universities than factories.

We were content to sit on a grassy bank, shake a few tins of nuts and bolts at the auto jumble or just earwig the conversations of others. Many were foreign bikers who invariably made better custodians of Britain's heritage. So often they had witnessed our destruction by redesigning a product in the pursuit of progress, often just for the sake of it. The new Triumph company seem wise to that mistake; the Bonneville and its derivatives are their best seller.

The other conversations I listened to by the beer tent were those of the Meriden workers. It is clear that they enjoyed working there, except perhaps poor Dobbin. I doubt he would suffer the same fate at the new Triumph factory: it is widely regarded as the most efficient in the world and they are too busy selling motorcycles to the Japanese.

Occasionally throughout the day I caught sight of John Rosamund. I was always pleased when I saw him surrounded by people. Sometimes I noticed him when he was on his own, nervously shuffling papers on his desk or more often, looking into the distance as the setting sun cast its golden rays on his motorcycles that had emerged from a factory, the success of which could have addressed so many of the problems that have been bestowed on future generations. But all this is too high-falutin for the Midland's industrialists whose prime concern was turning metal to motorcycles to provide for their families.

The park seat was getting hard and my leathers damp when I awoke from my pontification. I still had six miles to go and then I realised that this was the Surrey village of Ockley to which Mr Turner had retired. Famous now for celebrities and a super-model with unfeasibly large breasts, when Mr Turner arrived here in the late sixties, the echo of old money that he had encountered on the Gaffer's Gallop could still be heard.

On the 15th of August, 1973, the man who used to leap from the boardroom to test motorcycles at speeds of up to 100 mph whilst still in his tailored suit was enjoying retirement. He was now divorced and had custody of his three children, whom he set on course for careers at The Bar and as a Justice of the Peace, whilst Edward junior was at Harrow. The motorcycles he had made still held world speed records and although melancholy about the state of the nation generally, he knew there was nothing more he could do. His job was done. Never again would he 'do the ton' before lunch and on this particular morning he had to content himself with rearranging the furniture. In the afternoon he sat down in the chair in his front room and passed away. Many said that Britain would never see his sort again, but they were unlikely to have come across that son of a Derbyshire coal miner who picked up the torch and made it burn brighter than ever, something which would have made Mr Turner immensely proud.

I looked at the lines of Mr Turner's motorcycle sporting its empty petrol tank and then stood up to get my circulation going as the dew settled on the seat.

So what had this journey taught me? Clearly it was time for something deep and philosophical, but it did not come easy as I tried to massage some life into my sore backside. Well, I guess it has taken over 2,000 miles for me to conclude that no matter how flowing the lines of a Triumph may be, even they do not go very far if you forget to put petrol in the tank.

Sorry, but it's not *Zen And The Art Of Motorcycle Maintenance*.

NOTES

You cannot write a book in which you suggest you have been communing with the mates of Steve McQueen or discovered a plot to overthrow the government and not expect somebody, somewhere to cast doubt on your sources. So, here they are. I've included all of them (I believe).

If there are any omissions then I sincerely apologise. I've also included those that I have not quoted from directly, but the information they presented proved all but indispensable. Steve Wilson's scholarly *British Motorcycles Since 1950* deserves special mention here. Others are mentioned even where there has been the briefest reference. Having said that, where there are technical errors, they are mine and not theirs. This is not a technical book and where accuracy interfered with literary license the latter prevailed. There are plenty of books that can tell you the production figures for given models and I would be ill-equipped to add anything on which to judge a Concours d'Elegance. But then may be one day people will quote from *Travelling With Mr Turner* with the same reverance that I have quoted from *Travels With Charlie*... (ok, ok, I know).

Enter Mr Turner
Farewell Victoria (1933) by Thomas Hanbury White appears by kind permission of David Higham Associates.
General matters referred to also taken in part from the article titled *The Gaffers' Gallop* that first appeared in *MotorCycling* Magazine on the 15 October, 1953 and are reproduced by kind permission of Mortons Media Limited.
Travels With Charlie (1962 Penguin) by John Steinbeck

The Illusive Jerusalem
MotorCycling magazine, 15th October, 1953.
Edward Turner - The Man Behind The Motorcycles by Jeff Clew (1966 Veloce) is either referred to or quoted from directly and the use of such material appears by kind permission of Veloce Publishing Limited.
Graffiti appears courtesy of unknown artist

The Fertilisation Ceremony
Night Song Of The Last Tram (2006 Hodder Paperbacks) by Robert Douglas
Britain Since 1945 (2006 Routledge) by David Childs.

Return To The Imperial
Never Despair - Winston Churchill 1945-1965 (1988 Houghton Mifflin) by Martin Gilbert

BBC broadcast - John Betjeman (1937)

The personal papers of the late Bill Johnson

Triumph Motorcycles In America (1992 Motorbooks International) by Lindsay Brooke and David Gaylin

The Mint by T E Lawrence (Lawrence of Arabia) first published posthumously in 1955 by Jonathan Cape.

The Rolling English Road by G K Chesterton

Song Of The Open Road (1856) by Walt Whitman

BBC interview - Mr John Nelson

Edward Turner - The Man Behind The Motorcycles (2006 Veloce Publishing Limited) by Jeff Clew

The Open Road

More graffiti. Possibly same artist. Possibly not.

Harsh but fair comments about Stratford upon Avon appear by kind permission of Rough Guides

Our Mutual Friend (1908) by Charles Dickens

The Centre Of The Universe

British Motorcycles Since 1950 Volume 5. Triumph: The Company. (1991 Patrick Stevens Limited) by Steve Wilson

Personal exchange between Don Brown and the author

The Gold Plated Daimler – Time Magazine – 11th June, 1956

Triumph Motorcycles Since 1950 (1997 Haynes Publishing) by Steve Wilson

Quotes from *A Million Miles Ago* by Neale Shilton appear by kind permission Haynes Publishing Limited

The Verdict Of Peace (2001 Macmillan) by Corelli Barnett

Various quotes appear from the invaluable *Whatever Happened To The British Motorcycle Industry?* (1981) by Bert Hopwood and are reproduced here by kind permission of Haynes Publishing Limited

Although no direct quotes have been taken from *White Heat* (1997 Abacus) by Dominic Sandbrook, it is appropriate to mention its usefulness in reassessing the sixties. Equally, *Having It So Good* (2007 Penguin) by Peter Hennessy served a similar purpose in respect of the previous decade

Fast Classics magazine

The eulogy to the late Doug Hele was written and read by Norman Hyde and is reproduced here with his kind permission.

Spycatcher (1987 Viking) by Peter Wright

The Wilson Plot (1988 Heinemann) by David Leigh

The Benn Diaries (1996 Arrow) by The Rt Hon Tony Benn

Mountbatten (1985 Fontana/Collins) by Philip Ziegler

British Motorcycles Since 1950 Volume 5. Triumph: The Company. (1991 Patrick Stevens Limited) by Steve Wilson

Cycle World magazine (US)
Pax Britannica (Faber and Faber, 1973) James Morris
Private Eye magazine

Saturday Night And Sunday Morning
BBC interview - Hughie Hancox.
Various quotes appear from *Tales Of Triumph Motorcycles And The Meriden Factory* (1999 Veloce Publishing Limited) by Hughie Hancox and are reproduced here by kind permission
In Search Of England (1927 Methuen) by H V Morton.
The Uses Of Literacy (1957 Chatto and Windus) by Richard Hoggart
The Boys From The White Stiff by Mick Woollett *Fast Classics* magazine (Oct/Nov 1996)
Quotes from *A Million Miles Ago* by Neale Shilton appear by kind permission Haynes Publishing Limited
Cycle World magazine (US)
BBC interview - Les Harris.

Just Passin' Thru
The King's England — Yorkshire North Riding (1941 Hodder & Stoughton) by Arthur Mee
Motorcycle Cavalcade by Ixion (1950 Iliffe & Sons Limited)
The Verdict Of Peace (2001 Macmillan) by Corelli Barnett

Over The Top
MotorCycling Magazine, 15 of October 1953
Beveridge Committee On Broadcasting — minutes and society notes
Edward Turner - The Man Behind The Motorcycles by Jeff Clew (1996 Veloce) reproduced by kind permission of Veloce Publishing Limited
The House Of The Rising Sun (trad arr)
The Ace Café Then And Now by Winston G Ramsey (2002 After The Battle)
Hooligan Films (US)
Brittown — One World Studios Limited.

The Crown And Mitre
Office for National Statistics
BBC News.
Sociological Review - 'The Meaning Of The Coronation' by Edward Stills and Michael Young (1953)
MotorCycling Magazine,15 October, 1953
Edward Turner - The Man Behind The Motorcycles by Jeff Clew (1996 Veloce) reproduced by kind permission of Veloce Publishing Limited
Life Of Lord Halifax (1965 H Hamilton) by Frederick Winston Furneaux Smith Birkenhead.
National Geographic (US)
Cycle World (US)
Too Old To Rock 'n' Roll Too Young To Die (1976) — reproduced by kind permission of Ian Anderson of Jethro Tull and Tull Management Limited

It's Easy On A Triumph

Historie of Scotland (16th Century) by Hector Boece

MotorCycling Magazine 15 October, 1953

The Skye Boat Song (Speed Bonnie Boat) by Sir Harold Boulton, Baronet (1884)

Ring Of Bright Water (1960 Longmans) by Gavin Maxwell

Cath Raon Ruairidh

On The Road (1957 Viking Press) by Jack Kerouac

On Roads: A Hidden History (2010 Profile Books) by Joe Moran

The remarkable story of the relationship between Sir William Lyons and Edward Tuner was first revealed in an article titled *What If* that appeared in *The Classic Motorcycle* (Mortons Media Group Limited). It was written by Jim Patten following a discovery by Sir William's biographer, Paul Skilleter who enjoyed access to Sir William's private papers courtesy of his daughters Pat Quinn and Mary Rimell.

Edward Turner - The Man Behind The Motorcycles (2006 Veloce Publishing Limited) by Jeff Clew.

MotorCycling Magazine, 15 October, 1953 reproduced by kind permission of Mortons Media Limited

Classic Bike magazine (1st edition 1979)

Hooligan Films (US)

Extracts from the First Show Number of *Motor Cycling* magazine dated 12 November, 1953 are reproduced by kind permission of Mortons Media Limited

The Tiger Cub Bible (2010 Veloce Publishing Limited) by Mike Estall

William Makepiece Thackeray (1811 - December 1863)

Sir Henry John Newbolt (1862 - April 1938)

Two Years Later

The extensive quote from the timeless classic, *Jupiter's Travels* appears by kind permission of Ted Simon himself, (thanks again Ted).

Unmitigated England: A Country Lost and Found (2006 Everyman) by Peter Ashley

Small is Beautiful: A Study of Economics as if People Mattered (1974 Sphere) by Ernst Friedrich Schumacher